FLOWER GARDENING SECRETS

OTHER BOOKS IN THIS SERIES

Blue Ribbon Recipes

Traditional Home Remedies

Home Wisdom

The Old Farmer's Almanac Home Library

FLOWER GARDENING SECRETS

Sensible Advice from Seasoned Gardeners

Cynthia Van Hazinga

AND THE EDITORS OF

The Old Farmer's Almanac

OLD FARMER'S ALMANAC HOME LIBRARY
Series Editor: Sarah Elder Hale
Consulting Editor: Susan Peery
Copy Editor: Barbara Jatkola
Art Director: Karen Savary
Layout: Sheryl Fletcher
Cover Illustration: Sara Love
Illustrations, pp. 36–54, 65–92, 100–111: Karen Savary
Illustration, p. 121: Sheila Gilligan

LIBRARY OF CONGRESS CATALOGING-IN-PUBLICATION DATA
Van Hazinga, Cynthia.
Flower gardening secrets : sensible advice from seasoned gardeners /
Cynthia Van Hazinga and the editors of the Old farmer's almanac.
p. cm. — (The Old Farmer's almanac home library)
Includes index.
ISBN 0-7835-4936-9
1. Flower gardening. 2. Flowers. I. Old farmer's almanac.
II. Title. III. Series. SB405.V35   1997
635.9 — dc21   97-137337 CIP

Distributed in the book trade by Time-Life Books, Inc.

TIME-LIFE BOOKS IS A DIVISION OF TIME LIFE INC.

TIME-LIFE CUSTOM PUBLISHING
Vice President and Publisher: Terry Newell
Associate Publisher: Teresa Hartnett
Vice President of Sales and Marketing: Neil Levin
Director of New Product Development: Quentin McAndrew
Director of Editorial Development: Jennifer Pearce
Director of Special Sales: Liz Ziehl

TIME-LIFE is a trademark of Time Warner Inc. U.S.A.

Contents

Chapter 3 **The Pleasures of Perennials**

Chapter 4 **Sensational Flowering Bulbs**

Foreword

*T*HE 1790S, WHEN GEORGE WASHINGTON SERVED MOST OF HIS two terms as president, was not only the first decade of *The Old Farmer's Almanac,* but it also marked a turning point in American gardening. After the Revolution, Americans were determined to set their own style in things, including gardening, with a general movement toward order and structure. The first American seed houses were established at that time, writers began emphasizing native plants and garden designs suitable for the United States, and American gardens generally began to take on a new look.

In the forefront of these changes was the emergence of the American parlor garden — a scaled-down version of the more elaborate English manor garden. The major difference between parlor gardens and previous American gardens was that they were used exclusively for flowers and herbs. This distinction marked the first formal separation of flowers and vegetables in the gardens of ordinary Americans.

With its vast array of flowers such as geraniums, oxeye daisies, marigolds, violets, and black-eyed Susans, the parlor garden became particularly popular in New England, where, by 1800, the annual edition of the Almanac was a staple in most homes.

Because a fairly rigid division of labor sent men to distant fields and orchards to work on large-scale crops, women usually tended the gardens near their homes. They traded flower cuttings and seeds with friends and gleaned valuable advice on practical uses of flowers and herbs (medicines, dyes, insect repellents, and the like) from the pages of *The Old Farmer's Almanac.*

What Is *The Old Farmer's Almanac?*

First of all, it's the oldest continuously published periodical in North America. It was established in 1792 by Robert B. Thomas, a Massachusetts schoolteacher whose name still appears on the familiar yellow cover, and it has appeared annually on the American scene every year since.

Like any publication legitimately calling itself an almanac, it is also, as such books were known in ancient times, a "calendar of the heavens." In other words, one of its primary duties is to provide the astronomical structure of the coming year on a daily basis.

Perhaps what *The Old Farmer's Almanac* is most of all, however, is a vast compendium of useful and entertaining information. Its major subjects include food, gardening, home remedies, history, and odd facts that you just won't find anywhere else. Oh, yes, it has weather forecasts, too. We can't forget those.

In the past decade, during which the circulation has skyrocketed to include some 9 million readers annually, the Almanac has added a feature section covering current consumer tastes and trends — from collectibles to fashions to health news to money-saving ideas to, well, just about everything going on in America today.

So even though the Almanac is old, it is also brand-new every year. And in addition to being America's oldest publication, perhaps it has become, over these many years, America's most loved publication as well.

JUDSON D. HALE, SR.
Editor-in-Chief,
The Old Farmer's Almanac
(The 12th editor since 1792)

Introduction

*It is very difficult to write about flowers. I discovered this truth
only when I started to do so. . . . [I]n a very short space I had to combine
the descriptive with the practical — petals, in fact, with slugs; loveliness
with manure; lavishness with instructions for pruning. Successful
gardening is made up of all these things, and to be a successful
gardener one must also be a realist.*
— Vita Sackville-West, *Some Flowers*, 1937

I WAS WELL INTO THIS PROJECT, WRITING DOWN ALL I KNOW AND
have heard about flowers and how to grow them, when
I came across Sackville-West's declaration. She is quite right.
It's hard to find the proper words for the powerful but
ephemeral scents and colors of flowers and to be precise about
these issues, as every garden is truly a compendium of exceptions and
variations.

Every year the garden is different; every garden has its own character
and climate. There are always surprises. No other garden on earth will
be quite like yours, and only you can really know your own. You are

responsible for choosing and cosseting every leaf and flower, and you will come to know each one intimately — as we know our closest friends. You will make mistakes and have great triumphs — and they will be unique mistakes and singular triumphs.

And yet, paradoxically, it is all quite simple. Someone once remarked that civilization owes its existence to six inches of topsoil and the fact that it rains. Nature is on our side, and so are the multitude of wise gardeners who have gone before us. Since Adam and Eve, early converts to the division of labor, they have shown the way. Some have left us their note-books, some their names on plants, some their tastes and traditions. They have developed the gardening styles we honor, bred the plants we grow today, passed along the skills and techniques we depend on. How reassuring it is to know that we are not alone!

Garden wisdom — whether inherited from past generations, gleaned from neighbors and personal experience, or learned from great teachers and researchers — is a vast treasury, which we have tapped for this book. We revel in tips from friends and gardeners everywhere: botanists and horticulturists, soil and plant scientists, commercial growers and backyard gardeners, city dwellers and farmers. We have taken delight in talking to them and passing along their advice — with this caveat: trust your own judgment. What works in one case may fail in the next. Consider our recommendations, think them over, and give them a try if you're so inclined. One of the great things about gardens is that you have to wait only until the next growing season to try again, or to try something different.

Change is the very nature of gardening, and as the gardener, you will be both the agent and the object of change. As you plant and transplant, as you grow flowers and relish them, changes will happen in you and around you. Go forth and be joyful — be dirty and amused. For after all, the main thing about growing flowers is how flexible and forgiving they are — how often they will thrive and bloom madly even if you don't give them just what they fancy — and the great joy they add to our lives, from spring to winter, from daisies to orchids. As a poet once wrote, "Are not flowers the stars of the earth, and stars the flowers of heaven?"

Chapter 1

The Basics:
From the
Ground Up

Flower in the crannied wall,
I pluck you out of the crannies,
I hold you here, root and all, in my hand,
Little flower — but if I could understand
What you are, root and all, and all in all,
I should know what God and man is.

— ALFRED, LORD TENNYSON (1809–1892)

Stone Crop
(*Sedum, acre*)

NEW GARDENERS APPROACHING SEEDS AND SOIL, roots, and rockeries, for the first time, or even those with a good deal of experience who confront a new species or situation, should take heart: nature is on our side. Our best ally in the effort to fill our yards and our lives with glorious color and fragrance is the flowers themselves, for they live to bloom. Even if you plant all your bulbs upside down, fail to divide the irises, and never prune a single shrub, you are likely to be rewarded with beauty, for that is nature's intent.

Given sun, soil, and water, most plants will thrive. There's a bit of the farmer in all of us — for how short a time it has been since we all lived on the farm — and a lot of what goes on in the garden will seem as natural as smiling at babies.

Oh, there are a few tricks of the trade, and we offer them to you here, passing along the accumulated wisdom of our years and that of our neighbors. Gardeners love to give advice, and we are no exception. Our secrets are meant to be shared, and our wish is that you should enjoy every minute you spend growing flowers. Time cannot be better spent.

What's in a Name?

We like to think we are a rational lot, and during long winters and moonlit summer nights, we've had plenty of time and occasion to think about growing flowers. Growing them successfully, we mean.

The key, we believe, is to know flowers — their origins and histories, as well as their habits and behaviors. Their names give us a start, for when flowers were classified and when they acquired common names, those names were given, in most cases, by experienced observers. Thus, whether it's a botanist telling us that *Aegopodium podagraria* (the dreaded goutweed) has a wandering foot and will stroll all over your garden or a flower lover pointing out that Johnny-jump-up is an irrepressibly cheerful companion, the name speaks for the plant.

And then there's the matter of origins. Our gardens these days represent the world, and few of the plants we grow are native to where we live. When we walk among the flower beds, it's almost like taking a world cruise: there's Mexico, with the zinnias; there's Peru, with the four-o'clocks; China is represented by the forsythia, Turkey by the tulips, Japan by the bleeding hearts, and Australia by the strawflowers.

This information is astonishing and important. Knowing the geographic and climatic conditions under which a plant evolved and came to persist tells us what growing conditions it likes best. Some plants acclimatize readily, but many more can be made to succeed when we know their climatic heritage and needs. Once we understand, for instance, that tulips grow wild in Asia Minor, we can appreciate that they — and many other Mediterranean natives — require dry summers, detest irrigation, and relish well-drained, sandy soils. We can understand the limits of scarlet sage in our American gardens when we know that it is a native of Brazil, where it forms a shrubby perennial. The similarity of our own climate to that of parts of Japan and China explains why some Asian plants, such as peonies, hollyhocks, clematis, and wisteria, have settled right in and been accepted as a natural part of the landscape.

Know all you can about the flowers you want to grow. Know their names and origins, respect their needs and preferences, and they will reward you with the solace and inspiration of beauty.

How to Speak Plant Latin

*Y*ou don't have to delve very deeply into gardening to realize that those mysterious Latin (and Latinized Greek) names that appear in italics in catalogs and on plant labels are as important in identifying specific plants as your own name is in identifying you.

The translation of the scientific name of a familiar plant gives clues to its history and original uses. *Paeonia officinalis,* a member of the large peony family, is an old-fashioned single red peony that has long been in cultivation and once had medicinal *(officinalis)* applications.

Carolus Linnaeus, the Swedish naturalist, began the modern system of classification and Latin nomenclature in the 18th century. Linnaeus gave each plant a permanent set of names, drawn from early Greek and Latin efforts (some as old as Aristotle), that indicate genus, species, and sometimes variety.

In 1867, scientists began to formulate the International Code of Botanical Nomenclature, an intricate set of rules for identifying and naming all living things. The scientific name of even the most modern genetically engineered variety has this highly structured code and centuries of precedence behind it.

The list that follows is no substitute for a schooling in the classics but will help gardeners decipher catalogs and make good choices about plants. All terms are Latin unless followed by a (G) for Greek.

How to Pronounce Botanical Latin

Pronunciation of Latin plant names follows general English pronunciation, with few exceptions. To give a few examples:

Senecio cineraria =
seh-ne´see-oh sï-ne-ra´ri-a
(dusty miller)

Salvia officinalis =
sal´vi-a of-fi-shi-na´lis
(common sage)

Cardiocrinum giganteum =
car-di-o-cri´num ji-gan´te-um
(giant Himalayan lily)

Centaurea cyanus =
sen-taur´e-a si-a´nus
(cornflower)

-ae = long e
ch = k
c = s before i, e, y; = k before a, o, u
g = hard before a, o, u; = soft (j) before i, e, y

Accent: In two-syllable words, the accent falls on the first syllable. For longer words, it generally falls, as in English, on the second-last (penultimate) syllable of the word if that syllable has a long vowel (e.g., for-mo´sus), and on the third-last (antepenultimate) syllable if the second-last syllable has a short vowel (e.g., flo´ri-dus).

A Brief Glossary of Terms Commonly Used in Plant Names

acanthus thorn (G)
aestivalis summer
alatus winged
altus tall
amoenus harmless, charming
angustifolius narrow-leaved
arborenscens treelike
asper rough
aureus golden
australis southern
autumnalis of autumn
baccatus berry- or pearl-like
barbatus bearded or barbed
bellus beautiful
borealis northern (G)
brevis short
caeruleus blue
campanulatus bell-shaped
campestris growing in fields
candidus white
canescens grayish
capillaris hairlike
cardinalis bright red
carneus flesh-colored
caudatus tailed
cinnamomeus cinnamon brown
coccineus scarlet
cordatus heart-shaped
coriaceus leathery
corniculatus horned
cuneifolius wedge-shaped leaves
cyaneus blue (G)
dactyloides finger-shaped (G)
didymus in pairs (G)
digitatus finger-shaped
dulcis sweet
echinatus spiny, bristly (G)
edulis edible
elatus tall
erythrocarpus red-fruited (G)
esculentus edible
fasciculatus clustered, bundled
ferrugineus rust-colored
flavens yellowish
fulvus brownish yellow

germinatus twin
gibbosus humped, swollen on one side
glabratus smooth
glaucescens becoming bluish or greenish gray (G)
hastatus spear-shaped
heterophyllus with leaves of several shapes (G)
hirsutus hairy or shaggy
humifusus sprawling
humilis dwarf
inodorus without odor
junceus rushlike
kewensis relating to Kew Gardens
labiatus lipped
lacteus milky
laevigatus smooth
lanosus woolly
latiflorus broad-flowered
laxiflorus loose-flowered
leucanthus white-flowered (G)
lignosus like wood
limosus of muddy places
lucidus shiny
luteus muddy yellow
macrophyllus large-leaved (G)
maculatus spotted
microcarpus small-fruited (G)
mirabilis wonderful
nanus dwarf (G)
natans floating
nemoralis growing in woods
niger black
nitens shining
niveus snow-white
noctiflorens night-flowering
nyctagineus night-flowering (G)
occidentalis western
officinalis a formerly recognized medicinal
oleraceus from a vegetable garden
pallens pale
paludosus marshy
parviflorens small-flowering

patens spreading
pauciflorus few-flowered
pratensis growing in meadows
pubens downy
pumilus dwarf, small
puniceus reddish purple
quadrifolius four-leaved
quinquefolius five-leaved
radicans rooting
regalis royal
repens creeping
reptans crawling
reticulans netlike
riparius growing near a river
roseus rose-colored
rubens red
ruderalis growing among rubbish
rugosus wrinkled
sativus cultivated
scandens climbing
sericeus silky
setosus bristly
speciosus beautiful
spinosus with spines
stellatus starlike
stramineus straw-colored
strigosus stiff-bristled
tenuis slender
tinctorius used for dyeing
tomentosus like felt
tuberosus with tubers
urens stinging
vacillans swaying
velutinus velvety
vernalis spring-flowered
verus true
villosus with soft hairs
violaceus violet
viridis green
vulgaris common
xanthinus yellow (G)

From "How to Speak Plant Latin" by Mary Cornog, *The Old Farmer's Almanac, Special Reference Edition,* 1997.

Siting a Garden

It seems very simple, but it's the secret to success: if you are a reasonable person, you will not try to grow plants that are not suitable for your environment.

Think about your climate, your land, and your soil before you begin. Your climate is determined by annual rainfall, the heat and length of the summers, and the cold and length of the winters. Know your zone as defined on the U.S. Department of Agriculture's Hardiness Zone Map, found in every seed catalog. Use this map as a guide but feel free to experiment.

Think, too, about your particular microclimate when you are siting your flower garden. If you have a shady yard, choose woodland natives such as foxgloves and hepaticas, as well as other plants, such as hostas, that relish shady and partly shady spots. Lengthen the bloom time of a plant by putting it on a warm, west-facing slope. In northern climes, if you have a sunny, south-facing slope, that is the best spot to locate your garden. Ironically, though, a southern exposure is more susceptible to winterkill because of thawing and freezing during the coldest months. If you live in a warm region, you may be able to take advantage of a northerly slope, which will stay cooler on the hottest days of summer. It's worthwhile to get to know your property. Study it over time and draw your own conclusions.

Finally, become familiar with your soil. Sandy soil is good for drainage but not for holding moisture. Heavy soil, full of clay, compacts easily

and may prevent root growth. Choose plants appropriate for the soil as is or add whatever it takes to suit your flowers' needs.

❧ Don't try to garden under or near trees. Their roots reach out in a wide circle about the size of their leaf canopy.

❧ If possible, locate the garden near a water supply and handy to your house (you'll find it easier to spend time in it).

❧ Try to avoid a microclimate that's harsh for your region. In the North, this means a low-lying, frost-prone hollow that will collect cold air on clear, still nights or a northern slope that loses snow cover late in spring. North-facing sites not only are cool and shady but also tend to be moist. A gently sloping south-facing plot, which tends to be dry and hot, is just about ideal.

> *The first day of spring is one thing, and the first spring day is another. The difference between them is sometimes as great as a month.*
>
> — HENRY VAN DYKE (1852–1933)

In the South, the opposite is true: a gentle northern slope will need less water and stay cooler on the hottest days of summer.

❧ Consider the sun. If you want to grow flowers, you'll need the warmth and light of the sun. Most flowers need at least six hours (eight is better) of full sun a day to grow and keep growing. West-facing sites have morning shade and hot afternoon sun, so they're significantly sunnier than east-facing sites, which get cool morning sun and afternoon shade. You can change some things about your garden — such as the amount of water and the quality of the soil — but you can't change the amount of sun it gets.

❧ Walls, buildings, walkways, and even bushes hold heat in summer and cold in winter. Sections of the garden bordered by these elements will have more extreme climates than adjacent areas of the garden.

❧ If a plant doesn't thrive in one spot, move it; it may do much better in another.

❧ Aesthetics are important. Think about where you will enjoy your flowers most while you are outdoors, as well as from indoor vantage points.

> *Patience and perseverance are both important qualities for a good gardener, but a sense of experimentation is also really important. The best gardeners I know are always trying new things.*
>
> — Peter Hatch, Monticello, Charlottesville, Virginia

Gardening Tools

*There is always a tendency among beginners to overload with the
paraphernalia of their calling, whatever it may be. When the first
enthusiasm passes, and one becomes a careful and successful worker,
all that is superfluous is gradually dropped, and one realizes that
it is brains and not tools that make the successful gardener.*

— Ida D. Bennett, *The Flower Garden*, 1903

*D*on't load up your
shed or garage with
more tools than you
can keep in order
and good repair.
What do you really need to make
a garden? At the minimum, you
need the following tools:

❦ Hose with a decent supply
   of water or good
   watering can
❦ Pitchfork
❦ Hoe
❦ Trowel
❦ Rake

❦ Good sharp spade
❦ Wheelbarrow

*Don't try to work in unsuitable clothing. Easy, broad, solid shoes —
not any old run-down pair — should be considered as essential
as the spade, or rake, and skirts that clear the instep, and hang
comfortably. Waists with easy arm-holes and collar will
enable one to work with a degree of comfort that means
the accomplishment of an amount of work in a morning
quite impossible were one less comfortably clad.*

— Ida D. Bennett, *The Flower Garden*, 1903

The Seedy Side of Gardening

When you are growing flowers, it's helpful to remember their intent, for flowers do have a purpose, as does every living thing. Flowers bloom to set seed. They set seed to further their own kind. When you hold this simple concept firmly in mind, you will begin to understand how to manipulate (kindly, we hope) plants to get bountiful blooms.

GIVING SEEDS A HEAD START

Seeds started indoors can get a jump of four to six weeks on seeds sown in the ground. In regions with a short growing season, this means a great deal. In addition, in their vulnerable seedling stage, indoor plants have less competition from weeds. It's also less expensive to grow your own seedlings than to buy plants from a nursery.

🌿 Gardeners start seeds successfully in all sorts of containers and go to great lengths to coddle them at this vulnerable stage. Some plant in pellets, cubes, or peat pots; some use paper or plastic cups, wooden flats, or recycled cans. Our grandmothers used eggshells.

🌿 Moisture is the ruling principle at this point. Gardeners using moisture-wicking peat pots or paper bands must take special care not to let them dry out. It's also important to watch for the way the roots are forming. Seedlings grown in pots or flats lose some root strength when they are cut apart, and those grown in individual pots develop circular roots that take a good while to recover.

🌿 For strong, healthy seedlings, try soil blocks, available through garden supply catalogs. Container and growing medium all in one, each two-inch soil block is made of compressed potting mix, which is a bit wetter than most and contains a good quantity of fibrous material. Roots fill the soil blocks to the edges and then stop, so that when blocks are set out in the garden, seedlings become established quickly and without trauma.

🌿 With any kind of container, start seeds in a premoistened potting soil. Press them firmly into the soil, then cover them with glass or plastic (a plastic bag works well) and keep them warm until they sprout.

🌿 Above all, indoor seedlings need light — a sunny, south-facing window and fluorescent lighting if possible. Give seedlings 14 to 16 hours of light a day and keep them moist. Once they have a second set of leaves, they will need a weak solution of fertilizer as well.

> *Don't throw away the packets in which the seeds come.*
> *In addition to containing directions for planting and*
> *cultivation, they are excellent sources of information*
> *when the name of a particular flower slips the*
> *tongue and is wanted.*
> — *The Old Farmer's Almanac*, 1912

TRANSPLANTING SEEDLINGS: DO'S & DON'TS

❧ **Do** give seedlings a chance to toughen up before planting them out. They need a period of transition (about two weeks), called hardening off, to adjust to wind, direct sunlight, and fluctuating temperatures. On their first outings, seedlings need shelter and must come back indoors for the night. Later, when they have toughened up a bit, they may stay out in a sheltered spot.

❧ **Don't** let the seedlings overheat in a cold frame; never leave it closed on a warm day.

❧ **Do** handle seedlings with tender care.

❧ **Do** plan ahead. Have all supplies at hand before you begin.

❧ **Don't** transplant in the heat of the day. If possible, wait for a misty or cloudy day or late in the afternoon when the sun is low.

❧ **Do** poke a hole in loose soil and press the roots firmly in contact with the soil.

❧ **Don't** overwater.

❧ **Don't** allow the seedlings to be damaged by strong winds or strong light. Shield the young plants from direct sunshine for a day or so, or provide them with a cloche to raise daytime temperatures and speed growth.

The Four Essentials:
Moisture, Air, Food & Sunlight

Our calling as gardeners is complex, and yet in a sense simple. In the end, plants want only four things: soil moisture, air in the soil, food, and sunlight. All we have to do is figure out how to give them these four essentials. In general, this means providing irrigation and proper drainage, mulch, fertilizer, cultivation, and the right location.

SOIL MOISTURE

❦ Group plants according to their water needs. Don't put thirsty plants with those that need little water.

❦ To collect water when it rains, set shrubs and species with greater water needs in basinlike depressions.

❦ Water according to a schedule and during cooler hours, when evaporation is slower. Early morning is better than evening because the heat that follows during the day helps prevent fungal growth.

❦ If you're planning a garden, install a specific, efficient irrigation system such as drip irrigation. When you're replanning, consider retrofitting to supply just the right amount of water to each area of the garden. It's smart to take advantage of zoning and set separate lines into high-, moderate-, and low-water-use zones, supplying water to the bases of plants to encourage good root growth.

❦ Weed promptly, before invaders can steal water from the plants you want.

❦ Try using a water-holding gel near roots. Polymers or gels (such as DriWater) applied to the root systems of plants can reduce water waste. All you have to do is add them to the soil before planting and give the soil a stir.

❦ Mulch is miraculous. Pile it over plant roots (but not stems). Mulch conserves moisture as it cools soil and reduces evaporation. It also prevents weeds and slows erosion. As it decomposes, it improves the soil. Anything can be mulch: straw or hay, leaves, pine needles, wood chips, sawdust, bits of bark, pebbles, newspaper, black plastic, large flat stones. The best mulch for your garden is one that's readily available, inexpensive, easy to apply, and fit to look at.

❦ Work compost into sandy soils to retain water. Spread compost on top of the ground to protect roots from drying out.

AIR IN THE SOIL

❦ The better and less compact the soil, the greater its water-holding capacity will be. Be sure to amend the soil with compost or peat moss before planting any shallow-rooted annuals or perennials.

❦ Make sure you have earthworms in your soil. As they burrow, they are bathed in a mucus that stiffens the walls of their tunnels. The tunnels in turn aerate and moisten the soil.

❦ Compost improves soil structure. Worked in, it can loosen heavy clay soils for better root growth and drainage.

FOOD

❦ Commercial fertilizers contain nitrogen, phosphorus, and potassium. One main feeding per year, usually in the spring, is adequate for most flowers. Some plants require supplemental feedings.

❦ Earthworms produce more compost faster and more easily than any other organism. Their excrement, or casting, is organic humus, and every earthworm produces its own weight in casting every day.

❦ A top dressing of compost provides nutrients. When worked into the soil, it is a superior fertilizer.

Save soapsuds [not detergents] if you have a garden, for they form a very useful manure for flowers, as well as shrubs and vegetables. It is well to have a sunken tub in every garden where the soapy water can stand until required for watering.

— *The Old Farmer's Almanac, 1900*

SUNLIGHT

The amount of sunlight your garden gets will determine to a large extent what sorts of flowers you can grow successfully. Sun is energy, so most flowers, just like most growing things, like a good deal of sun; some plants, such as roses, like a great deal of it. This doesn't mean that you must forgo flower gardening if your yard is well shaded, but you will have to choose your plants with shade in mind — or cut down a few trees.

Before you begin planting flowers, evaluate the sunshine. Study the passage of the sun during the entire day and record it. Realize that it will vary according to season, cloud cover, and leaves on the trees. A sunny garden is one that gets at least six hours of direct, intense sunlight between 10 A.M. and 6 P.M.

- **Full sun.** Unfiltered, uninterrupted sun from sunrise to 3 P.M. or later.
- **Partial sun.** Five to six hours of full sun, with shade or filtered sun the rest of the day.
- **Partial shade.** Indirect sun (as it is filtered through a canopy of tree branches) with up to four hours of full sun or full shade per day. Or dappled sun all day.
- **Full shade.** Complete shade all day.

A Gardener's Prayer

O Lord, grant that in some way it may rain every day, say from about midnight until three o'clock in the morning, but you see, it must be gentle and warm so that it can soak in; grant that at the same time it would not rain on campion, alyssum, helianthemum, lavender, and the others which you in your infinite wisdom know are drought-loving plants — I will write their names on a bit of paper if you like — and grant that the sun may shine the whole day long, but not everywhere . . . and not too much; that there may be plenty of dew and little wind, enough worms, no plant-lice and snails, no mildew, and that once a week thin liquid manure and guano may fall from Heaven. Amen.

— Karel Capek, *The Gardener's Year*, 1929

Pesky Pests & Good Guests

Out in the garden, one thing is for sure: you're never alone. Although it's a fine feeling to spot a few good-size earthworms each time you turn a spadeful of soil, the sight of aphids feasting away on your asters and irises fills you with dread. Becoming familiar with the many residents of your garden is the first step in establishing a healthy balance of nature.

The garden that is so attractive to you also is very attractive to hungry beetles, borers, cutworms, and leaf miners. To them, a veritable smorgasbord awaits. But take heart: those pests are, in turn, very attractive to ladybugs, toads, spiders, and bats. Be a keen observer and let nature take care of nature as much as possible. If the balance tips too far in favor of your plants' predators, it's time to step in and take action.

Learn as much as you can about the various pests — how to identify them by sight and by the damage they do. (There are books with detailed descriptions of garden pests and ways to prevent, eradicate, or organically control their numbers.) Take a reasonable and responsible look at your options in getting rid of the invaders. Take measures to avoid future problems.

Following are a few ideas for effective pest control that don't rely on chemicals or expensive devices.

PESKY PESTS

Aphids
❦ Spray a strong stream of cold water to dislodge them.

Deer
❦ Scatter dog hair around the garden, or hang human hair in pantyhose or mesh bags in trees.

Earwigs
❦ Spread petroleum jelly around the stems of your plants. Earwigs won't crawl over it.

Rabbits
❦ Sprinkle powdered red pepper around the garden or on targeted plants. Rabbits are great sniffers, so that may keep them out.

Slugs
❦ Crush seashells and spread them around the plants. The shells also will add nutrients to the soil.

Squirrels
❦ Plant one or two cloves of garlic near spring bulbs in your flower bed, or sprinkle garlic powder or cayenne pepper on the soil when plants are ready to bloom. Repeat after rain.

GOOD GUESTS

Birds
❦ Blue jays, blackbirds, chickadees, purple finches, robins, sparrows, starlings, warblers, and wrens will keep your insect population in check. They will feed on aphids, cutworms, slugs, Japanese beetles, leafhoppers, and other pests. Include seed- and berry-producing **plants in your garden to attract** these birds, and provide bird feeders during the winter months.

Frogs & Toads
❦ If you live near a pond or have a water garden, you will benefit from the resident frog population. The frogs will voraciously consume cutworms, beetles, and sow bugs. Toads will eat ants, aphids, caterpillars, cutworms, grasshoppers, and slugs. A water dish, half-buried in the ground in a shady spot, will attract toads, as will a porch light left on at night.

Ladybugs
❦ Both the larvae and the adult ladybugs will feast on aphids (as many as 40 an hour), chinch bugs, mealybugs, scale, spider mites, thrips, whiteflies, and other soft-bodied insect pests. Attract them with pollen- and nectar-producing plants such as angelica, Mexican tea, morning glories, and yarrow.

Snakes
❦ Welcome garter snakes and other harmless snakes to your garden. They will prey on bulb-eating voles, mice, and other small rodents.

Beauty Over Profit

I recommend to any person, however humble his means, however narrow his land — if he must choose between beauty and profit, between flowers and shrubs on the one hand, and vegetables and fruit on the other, to have beauty.

I know this advice is directly opposed to the common opinion, which holds that all the land in the possession of a man not really rich, should be made "to pay," to feed or in some way support the bodily life of his family. But I hope I have already stated that which I shall urge more and more, that the chief consideration in managing any piece of land should be how it may give the largest amount of beauty consistent with necessary convenience and economy.

Potatoes and apples you may buy about as cheap as you can grow them, and you will buy them if you do not grow them, to keep body and soul together. Beauty can only be bought at the most extravagant price, and if it is not cultivated at your home, will hardly be bought; there is no physical appetite to clamor for it, and common economy begins by dispensing with it.

— R. Morris Copeland, *A Handbook of Agriculture, Horticulture, and Landscape Gardening*, 1859

Chapter 2

Annuals:
The Best
of the Brights

I come to the velvet, imperial crowd,
The wine-red, the gold, the crimson, the pied —
The dahlias that reign by the gardenside.
— *EDITH MATILDA THOMAS (1854–1925)*

Dahlia
(*Dahlia* spp.)

*T*HE FLOWERS WE CALL ANNUALS HAVE COME TO OUR GARDENS from all over the world and, like ambassadors and invited guests, are generally charming and adaptable. Most annuals are easy to grow and bloom in a wide spectrum of colors that range from the palest shades of pink and blue to potent reds, yellows, and oranges. They're usually long blooming and produce a profusion of flowers, since they are programmed to complete their entire life cycle and perpetuate their species in a single growing season.

Some annuals hug the earth, others soar to six feet or more, and some climb and trail. And they're just as varied in scent and foliage. Wonderfully versatile, they make great cut flowers and classic container plants, fill in gaps between perennials, dress up the vegetable garden, and can even be potted up in the fall to bring inside. And since we can raise them from seed, all this brilliance can be ours for the price of a few packets.

What Is an Annual?

The word *annual* is derived from the Latin for year and is used as an adjective as well as a noun. Simply speaking, an annual flower is one that completes its life cycle, from germination through flowering to setting seed, in one year or one growing season. Beginning gardeners may be content with that definition or even refine it to "any plant bought at the garden center in the spring that dies in the fall." But there are many exceptions to this rule and many variations.

The exceptions are partly due to climate, for many plants we grow as annuals in North America are perennials in milder climates. These include tender perennials such as geraniums and wax begonias, salvia, South African daisies, diascias, and verbena. They are often easy to care for, long blooming, and adaptable. California poppies, which most of us grow as annuals, may live for several years and attain great size in a warm climate with a dry, sandy soil.

Who's Laughing Now?
HA! And Even HHA!

A first glance at a seed catalog may give the impression that someone is laughing at the annuals. Actually, these cryptic acronyms are frost-tolerance classifications, a legacy from the British. They're also a shorthand way of describing a plant's growing habits.

HA stands for hardy annual, or a flower that completes its life cycle in one year. Sown in early spring, these relatively tough customers will mature and bloom in summer, set seed if you allow them to do so, and then die away. Hardy annuals can take considerable cold and will accept some frost, in some cases a surprising amount of it. Most can be sown directly into the garden, and their seeds actually germinate better if they're exposed to frost. In most places, the best time to sow the seeds is in the fall — in October in northern states and November or early December in mild-winter regions. Seeds scattered where you want them to grow as you do the last fall chores will beat the Memorial Day six-packs every time. Hardy annuals include calendula, California poppies, Shirley poppies, sweet alyssum, larkspurs, nigella, nasturtiums, stock, scabious, sunflowers, and sweet peas. As a rule of thumb, any self-seeder can be assumed to be hardy.

HHA stands for half-hardy annual. This crowd is intolerant of frost, among other things. They're a bit demanding; like to be cosseted in warm greenhouses until nights are truly warm; like loose, fluffy soil; and prefer plenty of water and fertilizer, given early and often. Half-hardy annuals also

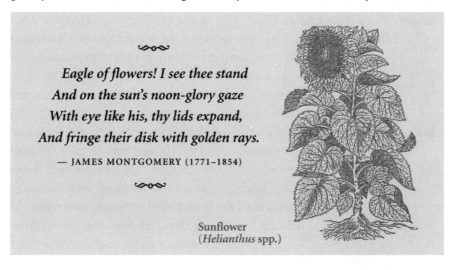

Eagle of flowers! I see thee stand
And on the sun's noon-glory gaze
With eye like his, thy lids expand,
And fringe their disk with golden rays.

— JAMES MONTGOMERY (1771–1854)

Sunflower
(*Helianthus* spp.)

germinate, flower, and die all in one year, but they require a longer period of growth than hardy annuals. To give them the best start, sow them indoors and then move them cautiously into the garden only when all danger of frost has passed. They are frost tender and don't like chill either. Half-hardy annuals include most of the summer bedding plants, such as begonias, cosmos, dianthus, impatiens, heliotropes, lobelia, marigolds, nicotiana, petunias, phlox, salvia, verbena, and zinnias.

TA stands for tender annual, a flower that originated in frost-free tropical climates and can't tolerate any frost at all. These flowers also dislike chilly days and nights and react by refusing to grow until the weather warms up. Some tender annuals discussed here are dahlias, geraniums (pelargoniums), love-lies-bleeding, and portulaca.

The Annuals We Love to Hate

Gardeners in a certain state of semisophistication have been known to look down on "ordinary" annuals. You've seen them sniff at zinnias, pale at the mention of petunias, go green at the sight of geraniums, salvia, lobelia, nasturtiums, and gladioli. Nothing could be sillier, from our point of view. Fashions in flowers come and go; taste is an individual matter. But gardeners need annuals, and knowing them, and how to use them, is a sure route to annual appreciation.

Even in the most meticulously orchestrated gardens, perennials can't do it all. Annuals add vibrant color, fill in spaces, and cover up dying foliage. They climb and ramble — in a hurry. They're perfect for containers of all sorts. Their strengths — long bloom and heat tolerance — make them perfect partners for many perennials.

And annuals aren't what they used to be. Each year, more and more unusual ones, and unusual varieties of more common ones, are available. Some of them are old-fashioned plants brought back into circulation, like the vintage zinnia mix 'Persian Carpet' and the fragrant old-fashioned sweet peas. Others, such as the amazing everblooming 'Supertunias', are brand-new cultivars. Some, like the balcony geraniums, have crossed the ocean from European nurseries; others, such as the smaller

Geranium
(*Pelargonium* spp.)

South African gladioli, have come even farther.

So don't be a plant snob. Try some new annuals and look at them with fresh eyes. Whether its a green nicotiana, a white sunflower, dark petunias,

> ∽o∾
>
> *Open afresh your round of starry folds,*
> *Ye ardent marigolds.*
>
> — JOHN KEATS (1795–1821)
>
> ∽o∾

single marigolds, or variegated nasturtiums, there's an annual out there ready to surprise and delight you. And that's just this year. Next year you can experiment again.

A Timely Trimming

For more flowers and a neater, bushier, prettier plant, it's essential to prune your flowers — whether you call it pruning, pinching, deadheading, or cutting back. Pruning is not just for shrubs and trees. Most annuals benefit from prompt pinching — removing the growing tip, usually just above the top full set of leaves — as soon as you set them out in the garden. In reaction, plants branch out, preparing to present more flowers later. Annuals grown primarily for their foliage, such as coleus, should be pinched all summer long to remove flower buds and keep the plant full.

To encourage repeat bloom, you must deadhead vigilantly. True annuals have slight root systems, as they don't store food for the future. They live to bloom quickly, set seed, and die. To foil this progression — to force the plant to conserve its energy for producing new blossoms as fast as the old ones are removed — you must stimulate it with constant picking. Cosmos, zinnias, marigolds, petunias, snapdragons, pinks, and salvia are some annuals that need continuous deadheading during the height of their bloom. This keeps them blooming. If you pinch pansies — or pick them promptly — they may bloom all summer.

Some annuals, such as cleome, calendula, amaranthus, balsams, and *Salvia coccinea,* are wanton seeders. Although you may want some of them to shed their seeds for next year's garden, a single flower head will do the job. Unless you want to find them all over the garden, be sure to deadhead them before seed heads form.

The Volunteer Garden:
Annuals That Self-Seed

Certain hardy annuals naturalize with particular ease, settling right in and acting like natives. Discovering which ones will do this in your garden adds an element of suspense to early spring. Unsolicited, tiny volunteer seedlings will be heartwarming and let you know that you are gardening in accord with nature.

Typically, annuals put out a lot of seeds and require vigilant dead-heading to look tidy in the flower garden. After all, it's their biological imperative to move smartly through their life cycle and perpetuate themselves. Allowing a plant to set seed does mean it will have less energy for blossoming (the rationale of deadheading), so wait until the second half of the summer to let seed heads form, but make sure there's enough time for them to mature before the first fall frost. Often it's sufficient to leave the seed heads on just a few plants, keeping the rest blooming and looking tidy.

Wind, birds, and gravity will do the rest, unless you choose to scatter the seeds in specific sites. (It's interesting to see where they will pop up, and sometimes it's the only way to get a plant to grow in an iffy spot such as a rock crevice.) Given the right conditions, which include a hospitable soil (if they fall in the garden, they'll be fine) and a light mulch, the seeds of hardy and half-hardy annuals will winter over and come up in the spring, already adapted to the garden situation.

Although some annuals do not come back true to color, some that do include calendula, cosmos, poppies, nigella, and morning glories. Self-sown annuals always seem to be hardier than packet-seeded ones, and because they get a head start, they are certainly earlier to bloom. All sorts of poppies are prolific self-seeders: try Icelandic in cold regions and Shirley, opium, or California in others. Nigella, or love-in-a-mist, is an old-fashioned favorite that is sure to reappear. Morning glories winter over in a mild year; so do larkspurs, alyssum, candytufts, and cornflowers.

Above all, enjoy your exuberant, impudent self-seeders. Don't worry about too much of a good thing; it's a lot easier to pull out what you don't want than to put in what you do. Give those volunteers a welcome wherever they show up.

Candytuft
(*Iberis umbellata*)

Saving Annual Seeds
for Next Year's Garden

With regard to seeds — some look like snuff, others like very light
blond nits, or like shiny and blackish blood-red fleas without legs;
some are flat like seals, others inflated like balls, others thin like needles;
they are winged, prickly, downy, naked, and hairy; big like cockroaches,
and tiny like specks of dust. I tell you that every kind is different,
and each is strange, life is complex.

— Karel Capek, *The Gardener's Year*, 1929

Seeds are mysterious. They tolerate conditions that their parent plants would never endure. They persist in deserts and drainpipes and survive boiling and freezing, indifferent to time. In all these things, they are extremely varied but also forgiving, for the life impulse is powerful and persistent.

When saving seeds from your favorite annual flowers, remember that hybrids are rarely worth the effort. Instead, save seeds from old-fashioned favorites such as nigella and flowers that have strayed into the garden from the wild such as zinnias and cosmos. Nurseries and seedsmen go to a great deal of trouble to isolate species and ensure high-quality seeds, so don't be surprised if your initial efforts have a lower rate of germination.

Save your seeds in a cool, dry place, and remember that the longevity of seeds varies greatly. Some seeds, such as lantana or heliotrope, will last no longer than a year in storage.

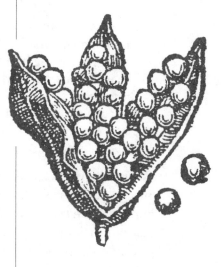

Our Favorite Annuals & Our Advice for Growing Them

Ageratum (HHA) *Ageratum houstonianum*

We've heard half-hardy ageratum, also known as flossflower or painter's brush, called "one of the annuals anyone can grow." All the more reason to love it. Certainly it is one of the prettiest blues in the garden, and there are also white and rosy varieties. It has feathery blossoms (the effect is of a fuzz of color) that grow in such profusion that the foliage is quite often hidden.

- Ageratum is not fussy about soil, but it should be well drained.
- If you cut off the dead blossoms faithfully, ageratum will bloom in full sun from early July to late fall.
- For early bloom, buy plants or start the seeds inside in February or March.
- We especially like 'Little Blue Star', a compact little fellow that grows only four inches tall, and 'Blue Horizon'.

Alyssum, Sweet (HA) *Lobularia maritima*

A trailing, low-growing plant that may never top six inches, sweet alyssum has profuse, fragrant flowers in dense clusters that attract bees. It's essential for covering dying bulb foliage and for summer edgings, especially in white, which has the same effect as a pretty lace collar.

- Easy to grow, alyssum blooms from seed in about six weeks. Try sowing it in the fall, as it does self-seed.
- The white varieties tend to reseed more prolifically than the purple.
- After about a month of bloom, shear, feed, and water the plant, and it will bloom again in sun or partial shade.
- Alyssum is not at all particular about soil.

Calendula (HA) *Calendula officinalis*

Shaggy, golden calendula is often called pot marigold. It's a European native grown originally as a potherb, for its medicinal properties and religious connotations (literally, Mary's gold). This is the old-fashioned herb our grandmothers dried to flavor soups and give them a rich, golden color. Hardy and happy to self-seed, it's a long bloomer in any climate and may bloom endlessly where winters are mild. It's that trait that gave calendula its name: there was an old belief that it flowered on the first day of every calendar month.

🌾 One of the easiest plants to grow, calendula thrives with very little attention. Once planted, it will produce sturdy orange and yellow blossoms as reliable as the sun.

🌾 Calendula prefers cool weather and full sun. It likes almost any soil.

🌾 Sow seeds in spring and again in July for fall bloom.

Candytuft (HA) *Iberis umbellata*

Native to the Mediterranean, including Spain, which gave it its scientific name, candytuft loves sun and heat. Its common name, which sounds like a sweet confection, also refers to Candia, another name for Crete. One of its old folk names, Billy-come-home-soon, suggests that it was commonly planted along cottage garden paths.

Candytuft is hardy and easy to grow. It quickly forms showy masses of soft, hairy leaves and flattened rounds of flowers in all shades of pink, rose, violet, and white, ever charming and unpretentious.

🌾 For a succession of bloom, sow just after the last frost, then again in a month, and a third time in late July.

🌾 Candytuft is not fussy about soil, as long as it is well drained. Don't let it dry out, or it will cease to bloom.

🌾 Thin the seedlings. Candytuft does much better if it's not crowded.

🌾 Remove dead flower heads to encourage growth.

Carnation (HA) *Dianthus* spp.

Carnations are hardy annuals (north of Washington, D.C.) that need full sun. No cottage garden should be without them. Annual dianthus blooms from seed in a single season on wandlike stems with bluish gray leaves. Gardeners years ago made a science of raising carnations from seed, using cattails and string to stake tiny flower stems, or even special carnation frames.

🌾 For early bloom, start seeds inside six to eight weeks before planting season. Plant them one-half inch deep.

❦ Move the seedlings outside when the trees are in leaf but before hot weather.

❦ Carnations need well-drained soil and a pH close to neutral, which may call for a dusting of lime. A little lime or ashes added to the soil between plants also will heighten the color of the blossoms and add stiffness to the upright stems.

❦ Give carnations plenty of water during the hot months.

❦ You may find that if you sacrifice the summer blossoms (pinch off buds), you will be rewarded in the fall with superior bloom.

❦ For huge blossoms rather than a profusion of bloom, remove all but the terminal buds on each stalk.

China Aster (HHA) *Callistephus chinensis*

Not true asters, China asters were found growing wild near Peking by 18th-century Jesuit missionaries. Sent back to Europe, they were named for their resemblance to the asters newly introduced from America. Grown at Versailles and in many other famous European gardens, they were subjected to extensive hybridization, especially by German horticulturists, and were sometimes known as German asters. They are very pretty and not difficult to grow, given good soil and full sun or even partial shade.

❦ Tall varieties may need staking.

❦ Remove buds from the side shoots, retaining the main (terminal) bud on each branch.

❦ China asters make wonderful cut flowers, but once cut, they will not rebloom.

❦ To avoid the fungal diseases to which they're susceptible, don't plant them in the same spot year after year.

Cleome (HHA) *Cleome hassleriana*

Tall cleome, or spider flower, has a charming, old-fashioned look growing with cosmos in a cottage-style garden. Among perennials, its blossoms look like clouds of white, blue, or pink. Cleome, native to South American jungles, does well in hot, dry spots and can grow to six feet tall. To get a hint of its exotic origin, smell the foliage — it's pungent and primal.

❧ Start it early or get seedling plants.
❧ Be sure to thin seedlings. Cleome needs a lot of space.
❧ Later in the season, the seedpods are attractive.

Cosmos (HHA) *Cosmos bipinnatus*

We rely on this old-fashioned pink, white, or crimson flower to put on a magnificent show. Although its name is from the Greek *kosmos,* meaning "ordered universe," it comes to us from Mexico. It is not frost hardy, although it will self-seed. The cultivar 'Sensation' dates from 1930 and has been a favorite since then. Plants may grow taller than six feet, billowing with ferny leaves and covered with as many as a hundred blossoms — plenty for many bouquets.

❧ Start cosmos indoors or out, but start it early so that it can attain its full height before frost.
❧ Cosmos may require staking or a few twig supports.
❧ It likes ordinary soil and full sun.
❧ It will do best during hot summers.
❧ Deadheading will prolong the flowering season.

Dahlia (TA) *Dahlia* spp.

Dahlias are tried-and-true garden performers that will fill a garden with color from midsummer until frost. There are hundreds of varieties in dozens of colors and sizes, and some plants bear as many as 40 or 50 blossoms a year if they're picked faithfully.

Dahlias were selected and hybridized by Aztec gardeners. By the time they were introduced into 16th-century Spanish monastery gardens, they were already far from the

Dahlias work well in landscaping for a mass of color, as a border plant, or in pots. They're equally versatile in cut form, used in bouquets and corsages as well as dried and fresh flower arrangements. And they're so much fun to grow.

— Bill McClaren,
   Alpen Gardens, Kalispell, Montana

original simple, daisy-like forms. Europeans found dahlias so exotic that a royal rivalry took root over their seeds. Empress Josephine of France planted seeds stolen from Spain, then banned dahlias when a member of her court grew stolen tubers. Meanwhile, Anders Dahl, a Swedish botanist, got hold of some seeds and began selective breeding, which the king of Spain rewarded by naming the dahlia after him in 1789.

Throughout the nineteenth century, both seeds and tubers were in short supply, and fortunes were made and lost dealing in them. At mid-century, New York City nurseryman Peter Henderson began producing his own seeds, launching the modern breeding furor that has led to huge blossoms (some as big as a dinner plate), stunning new colors, and all sorts of astonishing forms, including quilled, split, and notched petals; dahlias that look like cactus flowers and water lilies; and doubles, dwarfs, and two-toned blossoms.

❦ Growing dahlias is as easy as picking them. They like full sun, well-drained soil, and steady moisture.

❦ For fullness, pinch the tips after the first month.

❦ Pinch off the first buds for larger flowers later.

❦ In most areas, they are tender perennials that grow from tubers that must be dug up and "lifted" after frost blackens the foliage. (Cut off the foliage, hose off loose soil, and store them in vermiculite, sawdust, or peat moss in a moist, cool, dark place such as a root cellar or refrigerator.)

❦ Dahlias can be raised from seed, starting them indoors six weeks before the last frost.

❦ Tall varieties make great cut flowers. Dwarf varieties are ideal for container planting.

Geranium (TA) *Pelargonium* spp.

Native to South Africa, bold red, white, and pink pelargoniums (which we all know as geraniums) are probably our most beloved indoor plants. At home in containers of all sorts, as well as in garden beds, nothing beats them for color and cheer.

All geraniums have strong-smelling foliage, some with

scents so distinctive that they give the plants their names. There's a vogue for growing geraniums just for their scented leaves: lemon, lemon-rose, pine, peppermint, apple, orange, clove, cinnamon, and nutmeg.

❦ Geraniums like a mellow, loamy soil.

❦ During both winter indoors and summer out, pinch off shoots that may make the plant straggle.

❦ It's easy to root the shoots in moist sand (or even a glass of water) covered with a plastic bag.

❦ If you grow geraniums in the garden, dig them up before the first frost, pot them, and grow them in the house in a relatively moist room — the kitchen is best.

❦ Give them the sunniest window and a temperature of at least 50° F.

❦ If you have a lot of geraniums or a crowded kitchen, it's easy to winter them over in a cool cellar. (Like all plants, they need a period of comparative rest.) Lift the plants in fall, shake off nearly all the soil from the roots, and hang them upside down. Pick off all leaves that decay.

❦ In mid-May, cut back the withered stems to six to eight inches and plant them outdoors. They'll sprout new leaves and shoots and bloom in a short time.

❦ Worth seeking out: zonal geraniums, so called for the dark ring on their leaves; ivy-leaved geraniums, which trail; and multibloomers, which will flower out-doors all summer if you don't let them dry out between waterings (as you can with other varieties).

The geranium is the foundation of the average garden, and there is nothing more easily propagated. It will grow with the freedom of weeds with a little attention, and even under the roughest treatment it will do surprisingly well.

— L.J. Doogue, *Country Life*, 1905

Globe Amaranth (HHA) *Gomphrena globosa*

Globe amaranth is an increasingly popular annual with stiff stems and red, purple, or white flowers that look like large clover blossoms. It's also called bachelor's button, a nickname applied to several different plants. It's a native of India, introduced to England in 1714. Its round, long-blooming flowers do look like bright buttons.

- Sow the seeds outdoors in May. Globe amaranth likes almost any soil and full sun.
- For drying, cut the flower heads when the globe shape is fully developed (but not elongated) and the color is bright.

Impatiens (A) *Impatiens walleriana*

By some reports, impatiens is the single biggest seller at American garden centers and nurseries. It's odd to think that less than 75 years ago, impatiens was a rare tropical plant that no one had ever heard of. Carried to England (where they quaintly call it busy Lizzy) by plant collectors, it was grown in a few greenhouses. Even as late as 1960, however, few gardeners thought about trying to grow it.

A native of Zanzibar, in tropical eastern Africa, impatiens is a tender annual. In the wild, it is a rangy, sprawling plant with brick-red flowers, but it's always been a rapid, vigorous grower, quick to bloom. More important, impatiens answers the frequently asked question "What can I plant that will bloom in the shade?"

In the past 50 years, American flower hybridizers have greatly increased the color range of impatiens, which now includes a wide assortment of pinks, reds, and white. These days, almost everyone grows impatiens, and usually from plants started by professionals. This doesn't mean that a gardener should be afraid of starting impatiens seeds at home, although it is a bit tricky.

- The seeds germinate slowly, in about 18 days at 70° to 75° F. They need light to germinate, but they must never dry out.
- Plant in partial shade or in full shade where summers are hot.

Larkspur (Delphinium) (HA) *Consolida ambigua*

A lavishly blooming old-fashioned flower, larkspur's upright, branching stems give height to beds and borders. Spring-blooming spikes of white, blue, pink, purple, salmon, and carmine add drama to the garden.

❦ Sow seeds in fall or early spring. Larkspur prefers fertile, well-drained soil and sun or partial shade.

❦ Larkspur likes cool weather. In warm weather, keep the roots cool by mulching with dried grass clippings.

❦ For fall bloom, pinch off flowering stems after they have finished their summer bloom.

❦ Don't attempt to transplant large plants. It's better to grow larkspur where the seeds are sown, thinning seedlings to nine inches apart.

Love-in-a-mist (Nigella) (HA) *Nigella damascena*

Love-in-a-mist, which is also called devil-in-the-bush, has a wonderful clear blue flower that is well worth inviting into your garden. Its common name describes the effect of its pale blue flowers nestled in fine, feathery foliage. Its other name (devil-in-the-bush) refers to the interesting, spiny seed heads (good for dried arrangements) that follow the flowers.

❦ Love-in-a-mist has a taproot, so it's not easy to transplant.

❦ Sow seeds outdoors in fall or early spring. Thin seedlings to at least a foot apart.

❦ Once it's established, it will self-seed for many years, weaving politely among other flowers in the border.

Love-lies-bleeding (TA) *Amaranthus caudatus*

Love-lies-bleeding is an old-fashioned plant beloved by our Victorian ancestors but sometimes considered too gaudy for dainty gardens. It's also called kiss-me-over-the-garden-gate and, more descriptively, tassel flower or chenille plant for its tasseled streamers, which have the color and texture of Victorian plush. This is a tall, branching plant (almost five feet and sometimes straggly) with showy, drooping red plumes. In some forms, the terminal spike in each cluster is

longer than the others and whiplike; in others, it's shorter and thicker.

❦ Love-lies-bleeding is a hot-climate native that's easy to grow and flowers freely when days and nights are of equal length.

❦ Give this plant plenty of room in the garden.

❦ For good color, don't give it too rich a soil. Rich soil encourages rank growth and less color.

❦ For dried arrangements, harvest flower spikes before the seeds begin to ripen. The spikes dry well and last a long time.

Marigold (HHA) *Tagetes* spp.

Both French *(T. patula)* and African *(T. erecta)* marigolds are native Mexicans, where they were probably grown in gardens before Cortés arrived in the early 1500s. After colonization, they were sent to Spain and carried to monasteries in France and Africa, where they were called Mary's gold. By the time they reached northern Europe and made their way back to North America, few people remembered their actual origin. *Vick's Flower and Vegetable Garden* (1880) claims that the French marigold "no doubt, came from Peru or some part of South America, while the name of the African indicates its true origin." These days, although old-timers may speak of African marigolds, Burpee and other hybridizers have adopted "American" for dramatic *T. erecta,* the tall marigolds, and the rest of us have gone along.

❦ Marigolds are easy to grow from seed (as long as you give them at least 75° F to germinate) or from bedding plants. Starting them from seed gives you greater variety.

❦ They generally like full sun, except in hotter climates, where partial shade is better.

❦ Pinch off dead heads to encourage new blossoms.

Morning Glory (HHA) *Ipomoea purpurea*

Nothing is more ravishing than a fence or wall smothered in the heart-shaped leaves and fragile-looking trumpets of 'Heavenly Blue' morning glories. Here in our American gardens, morning glory is a tender vine; in its tropical home,

it's a rampant weed. We get a hint of this from the behavior of the thuggish, indomitable bindweed *(Convolvulus arvensis)*, which is nothing but a wild morning glory.

- 🐿 Morning glories can be tricky to grow. To ensure germination, the hard-coated seeds must be nicked with a file and/or soaked in warm water to soften them up. Sometimes morning glories will self-sow and, on their own schedule, do brilliantly.
- 🐿 If you have cool springs, start seeds indoors in peat pots, for they require a temperature of 75° to 80° F to germinate.
- 🐿 Another requirement for glorious bloom is restful nights. Like other garden timekeepers, morning glories need a good night's sleep and may not bloom if they are sited near a streetlight or yard light.
- 🐿 Given a good start — in warm soil and full sun — morning glories grow rapidly, and the reds, such as 'Scarlett O'Hara' and 'Crimson Rambler', are as wonderful as the blues.

> *I love everything about morning glories. The colors. I love their shape before they unfold. I love the tendrils. I file the seeds — just enough to break the coat — and soak them before I plant them. (They look like little worms.) Don't forget: they need a lot of sun. And remember, deer like morning glories more than anything else in the world!*
>
> — Delia Adams, West Shokan, New York

Nasturtium (HA) *Tropaeolum majus*

There are about 50 species of wild yellow nasturtiums, which are native to areas from southern Mexico to Chile. Their rapid growth and free-flowering habit make them great summer plants in our more northerly gardens. Today's hybrids range in color from rich, dark reds to orange, salmon, cream, peach, and yellow and come in both single and double forms. Some are fragrant, some trail and climb, and some have variegated foliage.

Both flowers and leaves are edible and have a peppery flavor that spices up salads. Once called Indian cress, nasturtiums were grown by our grandmothers for their edible seeds, which were pickled as a substitute for capers and ground for a sharp sauce like mustard.

- Sow large, easy-to-handle nasturtium seeds (good for kids) outdoors two weeks before the last frost, setting them exactly where you want them to grow (they prefer not to be shifted about).
- They are not at all fussy and will grow in any sunny or partly shaded spot, in soil that's not overly rich. Rich soil encourages leaf growth at the expense of bloom.

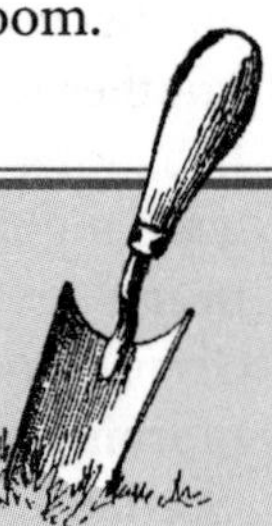

> *Nasturtium[s] . . . seem with endless good-nature ready to adapt themselves to any conditions of existence, except perhaps being expected to live in a swamp.*
>
> — Celia Thaxter, *An Island Garden*, 1894

Pansy (HA) *Viola* spp.

In an effort to set gardeners straight, a botanist once explained, "While all pansies are violas, not all violas are suitable for classification as pansies." Nonetheless, even non-gardeners know pansies by their sweet faces and innocent, old-fashioned charm. Pansies come in many different colors, from plain to blotched, and range in size from tiny to about four inches across.

- Grow pansies from seed, sown in fall or spring, or buy transplants.
- Protect them from hot sun.
- Keep them picked or pinched back to encourage continuous bloom.
- In regions with mild winters, pansies may bloom all winter long.

Petunia (HHA) *Petunia* hybrids

Life without petunias? Such was the gardener's lot before a botanical explorer picked a white petunia at the mouth of South America's Rio de la Plata in 1830. It was an immediate hit in Europe, as was the purple petunia found in Brazil a little later.

Today long-blooming tender petunias are among the most intensely hybridized annuals. The flowers are huge and doubled, fringed and ruffled, and come in dozens of shades of pink, white, red, yellow, and purple, as well as in stripes. Some of the best varieties are scented (especially the few open-pollinated ones), and others are semitrailing, useful for containers and window boxes.

❦ Start them indoors from seed or buy plants in spring.

❦ Some varieties need light to germinate, and the soil must be kept moist and at about 65° to 70° F.

❦ Once past the seedling stage, petunias are easy to grow, although they loathe cool, wet weather and heavy rain, which can beat the blossoms to a pulp.

❦ Give them sun, and more sun, and they will be delightful.

❦ 'Balcony White' is long flowering and looks snowy even in bright sunlight.

Phlox, Annual (HHA) *Phlox drummondii*

Annual phlox is, like its perennial cousins, a sturdy American native. In fact, it's a Texan, which explains why it thrives in hot, sandy soil and tolerates drought. Also called flameflower, Texas pride, and Drummond's phlox, this spreading, compact plant was discovered by Texas pioneer Thomas Drummond in the 1820s. It is a strong, erect plant, long blooming and slightly branching at the top, with large heads of individually large star-shaped flowers.

Drummond's phlox has velvety blossoms in glowing pink, rose, scarlet, crimson, lilac, and snowy white, some with dark eyes. Delicately fragrant, phlox might be described as having a wild-meadow scent — a natural, enticing perfume that invites sniffing.

❦ Phlox looks best planted in masses. It's good for the edge of a bed, for containers, and as a cut flower.

❦ When you're starting phlox from seed, remember that it needs dark to germinate; cover the pots or seed trays with black paper.

❧ When phlox gets settled in the garden, pinch it back to encourage full growth.

❧ It tolerates dry conditions and hot, sandy soil.

> *A good bed of Phloxes is a sight that dazzles the eye with its brilliance.*
>
> — *Vick's Flower Seed Catalog,* 1868

Poppy, Shirley (HA) *Papaver rhoeas*

The Shirley poppy is an improved variety of the wild European field poppy developed by Reverend William Wilkes, a vicar from Shirley, England, in the 1880s. Wilkes noticed a single poppy with a thin white edge growing among a mass of corn poppies. He saved some seeds and over the years isolated the lovely sport, creating a strain with wonderful shadings that he named after his hometown.

Old-fashioned and charming, the Shirley poppy has silky, wavy petals. The plants look their best covering a large area of ground, as they need light and space around them to show off their translucent petals and amazing range of colors. So subtle and various they're hard to name, the colors include salmon, coral, peach, ivory, crimson, rose, and blush, many of them edged with white, and the blossoms appear in both single and double forms.

❧ Shirley poppies are easy to grow from seed, which is the best way to start them, as they resent root disturbance.

❧ They are prolific self-sowers; the only trick is to recognize the tiny seedlings in early spring.

❧ Seeds sown in autumn will produce the earliest blooms the next year, from late May to July.

❧ A spring sowing of seeds will result in flowers from July on. Ideally, seeds should germinate and start to grow in cool conditions. Some gardeners sprinkle the tiny seeds over the snow in late winter.

Portulaca (TA) *Portulaca grandiflora*

Also called moss rose, rose moss, and sun plant, portulaca grows the world over. The showy type is a relative of wild purslane (which Yankee farmers used to call pussley), that fleshy garden weed that gourmets are now tucking into salads.

- If you have a dry, really sunny spot, shake out a packet of portulaca seeds in early spring or buy plants and set them out six inches apart.
- Portulaca is a low-growing plant, one that must be enjoyed on your knees. Or plant it on a wall near an outdoor sitting area or in containers.
- Self-sown portulaca may reappear year after year in sunny, seaside gardens.

Snapdragon (HHA) *Antirrhinum majus*

Snapdragons are named for the evocative structure of their blossoms, which have both upper and lower "jaws." The newer ones, such as 'Bright Butterflies' and 'Little Darling', include bell-shaped and azalea-shaped flowers. No annual repays the gardener more in effectiveness, and none is dearer to anyone who loves bouquets. Its tall spikes of bloom are sturdy and come in many colors, including deep crimson, deep yellow, wonderful orange-brown, creamy white, and pale pink.

- Snapdragons need a light, rich soil and a sunny location.
- They bloom best in cool weather, requiring nighttime temperatures of about 50° F to produce buds.
- To reduce the chances of rust developing, avoid overhead watering.

Stock (HHA) *Matthiola incana*

Old-fashioned stock, sometimes called Brampton stock, has a sweet, haunting fragrance. Old-time gardeners called it gilliflower. The plants have clusters of single or double flowers in cream, pink, lavender, purple, red, and white in one- to three-foot spikes.

- In mild-winter areas, stock should be planted in the fall.
- It needs full sun and warm nights to bloom.
- The tall ones are especially good for cutting; the smaller ones are invaluable in the front of the border.
- Do not thin seedlings; crowded stock blooms early.

Sunflower (HA) *Helianthus* spp.

People have always loved sunflowers, and now there are many wonderful new varieties. Some are doubles, some singles, some tall, and some small. Colors range from deep reds and rich golds to soft yellows and white chiffon, as well as some bicolors, all eager to grow into a wonderful living hedge or background screen or to be gathered for a dramatic bouquet. Sunflower petals can be added to salads for color, and each flower produces hundreds of seeds, which can be used for birdseed or dried and roasted for a delicious snack.

If you live in the Plains states, you probably know the wild sunflower, which has naturalized along roadsides and even in vacant lots. It's a robust, beautiful plant, free branching to six feet tall, which produces a profusion of three-inch golden "daisies" centered with a blackish brown disk. This sunflower is the state flower of Kansas, and its cultivars, distinguished by a single large flower at the top of its stem, make up the first basic type of garden sunflowers.

Plant breeders in the United States and abroad have developed sunflowers in a whole range of colors and sizes to suit every fancy. The second basic type of sunflower is *H. debilis cucumerifolius* (cucumber-leaf sunflower), a branching plant with up to a dozen smaller flowers per stem, which is better for cutting. 'Sunbeam' is the hybrid most like the Van Gogh sunflower. Its strong single stems have big flowers with deep golden-yellow ray petals and a disk of yellow-green surrounding a thin ring of burgundy and a green center. It blooms in just 60 to 65 days.

Dwarf bush sunflowers are multibranching and grow to just 2½ to 3 feet tall. They have huge four- to five-inch flowers that come in a range of colors from yellow and deep gold to bicolors in shades of bronze and mahogany over gold, all with a tufted, dark chocolate center disk. Elegant 'Italian White' sunflowers have crisp, cream-colored flowers about four inches across, with a gold zone and black center. They grow about five feet tall and are fabulous in big, casual bouquets.

Sunflowers are not only beautiful; they're also grown for their seeds, which contain as much as 30 percent of their weight in oil. Sunflower oil is easy to extract and very healthful. Sunflowers raised for their seeds have huge, heavy heads up to 12 inches across and grow about 12 feet tall. Birds and squirrels love the seeds and may clean out a sunflower head while it is standing in the garden.

❦ All sunflowers grow best in full sun, and no plant is easier to grow.

❦ Scatter seeds on open ground and rake in lightly. The seeds will germinate in 7 to 14 days.

❦ Seedlings should be thinned when they are about eight inches tall. Unlike most tall plants, sunflowers don't mind company and grow well with as little as two feet between them.

❦ They accept transplanting when about six to eight inches tall, as long as you move them with a little ball of earth.

Some years back we met a sunflower enthusiast who had coaxed a prize plant to grow 20 feet tall. When asked what his secret was, he smiled and said, "I just throw the seeds down and run like hell." While this trick may work, it's just as rewarding to grow some of the smaller sunflowers in your garden — varieties that hover around six feet, with multiple stems and dozens of vase-size blossoms. They're becoming wildly popular and make the garden sing in the fall. For best results, plant sunflowers where you want them to grow when the soil is warm and nights are predictably above 55° F.

— *The Old Farmer's Almanac*
Gardener's Companion, 1996

Sweet Pea (HA) *Lathyrus odoratus*

Deservedly among the most popular flowers, the sweet pea delights us with its fragile, seductive fragrance and dainty, irresistible flowers in a wide range of colors, from bright to pastel. Its scent has been likened to that of honey and orange blossoms. The flowers make great bouquets and boutonnieres.

In their native Sicily, wild ornamental peas have weak stems and an intense scent. The sweet pea was first introduced to England in 1700, when a monk from Sicily sent seeds to a fellow botanist, and ever since it has been a much-loved flower of the people, both in England and America, at home in cottage borders and fine gardens, in vases and nosegays.

The first sweet pea with frilled petals appeared in Countess Spencer's garden at Althorp Park at the beginning of the 20th century (Princess Diana is her direct descendant), and some of the prettiest old-fashioned cultivars are still called Spencers. Since then, there have been many new cultivars, and for many years the development of a new sweet pea was newsworthy. Some say that the popularity of sweet peas was the main factor in establishing California as a major flower-seed-growing district. Modern hybrids have stronger stalks and larger blooms, and breeders now offer varieties with both old-fashioned perfume and heat resistance. The cultivation of sweet peas may present a challenge until you get the hang of it.

🌱 Sweet peas bloom most happily with their heads in the sun and their roots in cool, moist soil. They are quite hardy.

🌱 They grow from large, easy-to-handle pealike seeds and have the usual requirements of good soil and full sun. Before planting, file or chip the seed coat slightly and/or soak in warm water for at least two hours.

🌱 They are slow to germinate and must be kept cool. Whenever possible, plant low-growing annuals in front of them to shade their roots.

🌱 Early sowing is one of the secrets of success with sweet

peas. In Zone 7 or colder, plant them in spring as early as the soil is dry enough to work.

- Plant some five inches deep and cover up with about two inches of soil. As they grow, hoe more soil up to them.
- In the coldest parts of the country, get a jump on the season by starting sweet peas indoors in three-inch pots. Harden them off for at least a week, then set them out in the garden when the soil can be worked.
- If you garden in Zone 8, 9, or 10, plant sweet peas in late fall so that they can develop and bloom in late winter and early spring. Sown in August, they'll bloom in December.
- Don't make the mistake of planting sweet peas in the same spot for too many years in succession. Just like English peas, they may exhaust the soil, leaving you with "pea-poor soil."
- Except for the bush types, sweet peas are climbers. Give them good support (at least six feet). Some varieties, in some climates, may climb to nine or ten feet. If you don't have a fence or trellis, provide brush or chicken wire. Bush types (dwarf sweet peas) have no climbing tendrils but form freestanding clumps. Petite varieties, which grow only about a foot tall, are good for containers, window boxes, or hanging pots.

Tobacco, Flowering (HHA) *Nicotiana alata*

Flowering tobacco is enjoying a new popularity and may even be habit-forming, especially among those who linger in fragrant night gardens. Sometimes called jasmine tobacco or nicotiana, it is a long-flowering, large-leaved tender annual that is easy to grow and frequently self-seeds. The plants form basal rosettes of downy leaves that are a bit sticky, and the slender flower stalks hang with tubular blossoms like flaring trumpets. The flowers are two to four inches long and come in shades of white, pink, red, and lime green. When they open in early evening, they give off a fabulous scent that lures moths and butterflies. White varieties seem to be the most fragrant.

Mature plants are about three to four feet tall and make a great statement in the garden, bested only by woodland tobacco (*N. sylvestris*), a six-foot-tall scene stealer that may leave garden visitors spellbound. (*Sylvestris* means "of the woods.")A late-19th-century seed catalog recommended planting nicotiana in the center of a bed of evening flowers under the parlor window. Another catalog advises cutting them for bouquets to set in a dim corner.

❦ Sow nicotiana directly in the garden or start seeds indoors six to eight weeks before the last frost.

❦ Nicotiana grows well in almost any soil but appreciates a bit of lime and potash.

Verbena, Sweet (HHA) *Verbena* spp.
Verbena is an old favorite for color and continuous bloom from June to heavy frost. Nostalgic *Verbena* × *hybrida*, sometimes known as rose vervain or rose verbena, is the verbena we remember from our grandmothers' gardens. It's an easy, trailing plant, usually pink, magenta, or scarlet in color, and forms a three-inch nosegay of bloom. (Children everywhere learn to nibble on verbena clusters, tasting their sweet nectar.) Tall verbena is a great "see-through" plant, good for the front of the garden.

❦ Verbena tolerates drought and baking heat, and even prefers to dry out a bit between waterings (after all, it's a native of South America).

❦ Don't feed it too generously.

❦ Grow verbena as a low border for your garden, keeping the old flower heads pinched.

❦ Verbena is a bit difficult to grow from seed, having a poor germination rate, largely because of the seeds' waxy outer coat. In time, moisture and oxygen penetrate the coat, but do give the seeds every advantage, even bottom heat (about 65° F) and shade to prevent temperature fluctuation. You might prefer to pick up a six-pack of seedlings at the garden center or take a root cutting.

Zinnia (TA) *Zinnia elegans*
The zinnia, a native of Mexico that was grown by the Aztecs, is one of our best and favorite old annuals. After the driest summer, who has not said with a sigh, "Well, at least the zinnias were good." Throughout the 19th century, the single

variety was called youth-and-old-age. When the first doubles (*Z. elegans*) arrived by way of Europe at the turn of the century, they were hailed as a new plant and compared to the dahlia, which they do resemble.

Nothing beats the zinnia for bold brilliance, whether glowing orange, red, or pink or shining white. We especially like (butterflies do, too) 'Persian Carpet', an old-fashioned variety that has tightly overlapping petals with pointed tips and comes in lovely shades of cream, yellow, chestnut, and deep red.

These days, fashionable gardeners are wild about the chartreuse zinnia 'Envy', which blooms in light shade as well as sun. It looks best with dark petunias or other flowers suffused with color. Another good variety is the exuberant *Z. angustifolia*, with its simple daisy-like flower. It has a loose, informal habit, producing billowing mounds of cheerful color, and stands up to drought, humidity, heat, and mildew.

🌱 Unless you live in South America, zinnias have to be started indoors six to eight weeks before the weather warms up so that they will have time to bloom madly before frost.

🌱 The secret to starting them is plenty of air and not much heat; keep the pots at about 60° F (no hotter).

🌱 You might do well to start them outdoors in a little clump and then transplant them. A stiff breeze will do them good as they are getting to the transplant stage.

I love [zinnias'] color — they give the most lift — they really suit me. I usually start them inside and plant them in a bed near the vegetable garden, separate from the flower garden. They make a massive burst of color there, and I don't feel bad about cutting them.

— Ellen Mitchell, Loudon, New Hampshire

❦ Ever notice that the first flowers to bloom on each plant aren't especially remarkable? Pick 'em quick and pinch the plant, too. Give it a dose of fertilizer (although reasonably fertile soil, as long as it is well drained, is good enough for zinnias) and plenty of water, then stand back and watch them grow

The Pleasures of Gardening

It is for the love of a garden, that the most powerful influence is exerted in attracting men to their homes, and for this very reason, every possible encouragement that is given to promote a taste for ornamental gardening, secures an additional guarantee for domestic felicity, and the unity, morality, and happiness of the social circle. Nor must it be forgotten that as a recreation it conduces materially to health, advances intellectual improvement, softens the manners, and subdues the tempers of men.

Of all embellishments, flowers are the most beautiful, and man alone, of all the sentient tribes, seems capable of deriving enjoyment from them. With infancy the love for them commences; throughout the period of adolescence and youth, it continues unabated, increasing with our years, and becoming a great and fertile source of comfort and gratification in our declining days. . . .

In the growth of flowers, from the first tender shoots putting forth from the earth, through all the changes which they undergo, to the period of their utmost beauty, man will do well to behold and contemplate the wonderful process of creative wisdom and power. . . .

But after all, it is needless for us to expatiate on such a subject, for the pleasures of gardening are not derivable from elaborate treatises, nor very easily communicable. To be properly appreciated, they must be diligently sought after, and when once tasted, the mind will rarely become satiated, but will rove as the bee, from flower to flower, in search of nutritive and delicious sweets, extracting from each successive object, fresh stores of wisdom and delight, till at length it succeeds in amassing that which most truly constitutes the wealth of man — a fund of knowledge of the great Creator's works.

— William Valk, *The Horticulturist*, 1852

Chapter 3

The Pleasures of Perennials

Where are the dear, old-fashioned posies,
Quaint in form and bright in hue,
Such as grandma gave her lovers
When she walked the garden through?

— *ETHEL LYNN BEERS (1827–1879)*

Foxglove
(Digitalis purpurea)

*W*HEN WE THINK OF A FLOWER GARDEN, OUR IMAGE IS usually that of an English cottage garden or flower border, generously laid out in drifts of color with spires, fans, and mats of flowers, many of them aristocratic old-fashioned perennials, beautiful in their variety and continuously abloom.

Of course, our country does not share a climate with England, except perhaps in the Pacific Northwest, but there's nothing wrong with this ideal or any other, whether it's a grand landscape or a cozy backyard bed. What's important is that it be a retreat and that it provide an escape for the consideration of beauty, free of fashion.

But gardens have fashions, and it's strange to think that for some time, some years ago, perennial gardens fell out of favor. The rage for growing exotic annuals, usually in formal-bed formations, followed their discovery in the far corners of the world. New and glamorous tender annuals such as zinnias, marigolds, petunias, and geraniums had never been seen before, and their bold colors dazzled Victorian gardeners, who cultivated them madly. They grew them under glass, in carpet beds, in formal borders, forgetting for a time the sweet old cottage gardens their mothers and grandmothers had loved.

Of course, it didn't take long for a reaction to set in. Both William Robinson, the Irish garden designer, and his disciple Gertrude Jekyll, railed against beds of annuals and spearheaded a return to perennial gardens. **American gardeners** followed suit — with variations. In our country's wildly different climates, with our incredible legacy of native plants, it was inevitable that American perennial gardens would be unlike any others. We have desert gardens, winter gardens, water gardens, woodland gardens, and many other sorts, and we are still finding our way, getting inspiration from the plants and gardens of the past, adopting compatible cultivars from gardens around the world, and learning that it is the process of gardening that is the perennial pleasure.

The Variable Life Spans of Perennials

We've heard gardeners define a perennial as "a plant, which if it lived, would grow year after year." Beginning gardeners often assume that *perennial* means forever. In fact, it does not; the life span of perennial plants is variable, and a "relatively long-lived" perennial flower may live from three to five years.

All the life span classifications are more approximate and more misleading than we may suppose. Annuals often live longer than one year if we check their flower production to prolong their vegetative season. Thus, we can grow annuals as biennials and biennials as triennials, although repeat flowering may prove to be a greater drain on plant vigor than natural seed production.

Similarly, some perennials behave like annuals. Helianthus, the perennial sunflower, is perennial only by courtesy; no part of the plant lives longer than a year. Some perennials, especially trees, live extremely long lives: the giant redwoods are at least several thousand years old.

But what of other flowers? An individual carnation may live for six or seven years, but if we take cuttings from it, we can prolong its life indefinitely. Lavender lives on if we prune it, and California poppies, which most botanists see as annuals, may live for several years, as long as a perennial, if they find a sympathetic home on a dry, sunny slope. Some plants, such as sweet William, are perennial in the wild but behave as annuals or biennials in the garden.

Starting perennials from seed takes patience. Sometimes seeds sown in August don't show signs of life until next May. Be prepared to let Nature

ᏗᎣᏗ

Be patient, O be patient! Put your ear against the earth;
Listen there how noiselessly the germ o' the seed has birth.
How noiselessly and gently it upheaves its little way
Till it parts the scarcely broken ground,
and the blade stands up in day.

— WILLIAM COLES, *THE ART OF SIMPLING*, 1656

ᏗᎣᏗ

take her course, and for the best results, follow her lead. If a flower naturally sheds its seeds about its own feet in autumn, plant seeds at the same time of year. Sow plenty, making allowances for those that are taken by birds and insects and others that fail to germinate because of overly wet weather, because they have been allowed to dry out, or because they have been planted too deep. The beginning of life is a delicate matter, but time and Nature are on the side of survival.

Most records of plant life spans are largely anecdotal and speculative. Keep in mind that if a plant rated a true perennial should perish for no apparent reason, it may have lived out its life span and died peacefully of old age. Make a note of it; perhaps you can contribute to the historical record and further our understanding of this aspect of plant life.

The Vigilant Gardener: Tips for Maintenance

There's virtue in maintenance — and pleasure, too — because it forces you to really look at your flowers. Is taking time and care its own reward? We think so.

Gardening, especially growing perennial flowers, is a matter of a few routine tasks, such as weeding and watering, and then a bit more. One wise gardener we know has called it the "layer of craft." (It may even be art.) Everyone brings a different eye to the contemplation of a plant — sees it a bit differently and makes personal decisions as to what it needs. Does it need deadheading, pruning, staking? Does it look crowded, need division? Do you like those seed heads or hate them? It's up to you. Your decisions will shape the character of your garden.

Our single best tip for garden maintenance is plan ahead. Think about your plants and your garden before you touch a trowel. Design the garden and choose the plants to fit the level of maintenance you — or anyone who'll be helping you — can and will deliver. If you know your plants' needs for soil, sun, and water and its habits (Does it tower, flop, weave? Is it invasive? When does it bloom?), you will be well prepared to minimize its care.

THE IMPORTANCE OF WEEDING

Some love it, some hate it, but like it or not, weeding is a crucial part of garden maintenance, for weeds, whatever they are, are always with us. Try to see weeding as a meditative act, counsels a meticulous gardener we know. Getting down to weeding is getting down to earth with your plants, at their own level. You're like a doctor making rounds, checking in with each and every bedridden individual, taking a close look at each plant's condition, noting changes, looking for any signs of decline or illness, celebrating growth and development.

> ❧
>
> *Gentlewomen,*
> *if the ground be not*
> *too wet, may doe themselves*
> *much good by kneeling*
> *upon a Cushion*
> *and weeding.*
>
> — WILLIAM COLES,
> *THE ART OF SIMPLING*, 1656
>
> ❧

❧ **When to Weed** Weeding is a commitment, not a sometime thing. If you like schedules, weeding on a weekly schedule makes sense. Otherwise, train yourself to respond to a clear morning with a sunny session of weeding, or just do it as often as you can. In the gardener's year, there are two crucial weeding times: spring and early fall.

Spring is the heaviest weeding season, especially early spring, when hardy weed seeds that have wintered over spring to life — along with everything else in the garden. Recognizing weeds in the seedling stage is a challenge, especially for the beginning gardener. Diagnosis is to some degree a matter of experience. Our rule of thumb is if it looks important, it probably is. If that mysterious seedling turns out to be a dandelion, you can always pull it out next week.

Even if you hate to weed and rarely get around to it, make an effort to pull weeds before they go to seed. Remember this old saying: "One year's seeding makes seven years' weeding."

❧ **How to Weed** The most important thing about weeding is thoroughness. If you bother to weed at all, do it well. Nearly all of the most notorious weeds can reproduce from a tiny scrap of root left in the soil and will thrive from the stimulation of loosened earth. Using your fingers or your favorite weeder, dig deep, getting your fingers into the crown of the plant. Get the roots — or you might just as well have stayed in your hammock.

ENCOURAGE REPEAT BLOOM

Deadheading, removing spent flower heads or stalks, is the secret to encouraging repeat bloom. Deadheading prevents the development of seed heads, quite apart from keeping the garden looking tidy, for if seeds are allowed to develop, the production of flowers will cease or certainly be reduced. Just how to do it? There are three ways, which have been called snip, shape, and shear.

Snipping off dead flower heads is the method to use with plants with distinct flower stalks that bloom over a long period of time. It's a precise, deliberate task, removing each spent bloom just above the closest node. Buds of the next blossoms will develop at this point, at the leaf axil. Re-blooming perennials that benefit from fastidious snipping include yarrow, bellflowers, baby's breath, lobelia, phlox, salvia, verbena, and feverfew. Continuously blooming perennials depend on snipping, too, especially purple coneflower, sunflowers, rose campion, and balloon flower. Others, such as peonies, hostas, hellebores, daylilies, and coral-bells, look better if you prune them of dead blossoms.

Plants that have a bushy habit and produce many blossoms that all fade at about the same time benefit from *shaping*. Do this with sharp hedge shears, cutting the plant back by one-third to shape it into an agreeable mound, or muffin shape. Plants to shape include blue star and baptisia.

Low-growing plants with a tendency to get leggy and sparse call for ruthlessness. These plants, which include lady's-mantle, cat-mint, and hardy geraniums, should be *sheared* to the ground, then mulched and fertilized. This will promote quick regrowth.

Yarrow
(*Achillea* spp.)

STAKING: A QUESTION OF SUPPORT

Many full-flowering plants need support, but just as with underpinnings designed for full-figured fashion, it should be unobtrusive, discreet — if possible, even invisible. If plant supports are well placed, you won't notice them; if they're awkwardly installed, you'll see them all too well.

To stake perennial plants (and also sprawling annuals such as cosmos and baby's breath), use plant support rings (often called grow-throughs), bamboo stakes, or pieces of twiggy brush (called pea-staking). Whichever method you choose, make every effort to avoid tying the plants conspicuously. The effect of "plants in bondage" is not desirable.

Grow-throughs are the best choice for plants that really need season-long support and have a bushy habit that will hide the support. Peonies are a good example, and the old-fashioned peony ring has stood the test of time. Modern plant support rings, crosshatched and mostly made of light-weight metal, do the same job. Plants that benefit from this sort of attention include blue star, baptisia, campanula, globe thistle, baby's breath, balloon flower, purple coneflower, and large ornamental grasses.

Slim bamboo stakes, best dyed green, are ideal for plants with strong single stems that need support for only a short period of time. Set the slender stake close to the stem, cut it a bit shorter than the stem, and tie it to the stem with green or natural-colored twine. A shorter length of bamboo, angled into the ground at the base of the plant, can support shorter plants. This staking method is best for hollyhocks, delphiniums, foxgloves, sunflowers, lilies, and thalictrums.

Staking plants with twiggy brush is called pea-staking for its time-honored use in the pea patch. It is used primarily for plants that threaten to crack open, such as veronica, but also may be used for ramblers such as perennial sweet peas. Cut some twiggy branches or save them when you are pruning. Butterfly bush and red- or yellow-stemmed dogwood are good sources. Use this method of support for perennial geraniums, Bowman's-root, gooseneck loosestrife, and autumn clematis.

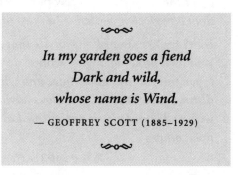

In my garden goes a fiend
Dark and wild,
whose name is Wind.

— GEOFFREY SCOTT (1885–1929)

YOU *CAN* BE TOO RICH

It's true: some perennials like it lean and light. Many sun-loving, drought-resistant plants that have evolved to succeed in lean soils suffer and decline if you give them too rich a bed. Yarrow, lupines, and coreopsis are among them; they all grow best where the soil's not rich. If you overfeed them, they tend to become soft and succulent and may even be too spoiled to stand up straight. If a plant is susceptible to disease, such as phlox, soft overfed tissue is more vulnerable to mildew and other afflictions.

Rich soil gives an unwelcome boost to plants such as bee balm, which spread stoloniferously (i.e., via an aboveground, horizontal shoot that forms roots at each node). Instead of standing its ground and blooming, bee balm will roam and range, blooming less. Excess soil fertility also can make some plants less colorful: amaranth may lose its glowing red; gray-leaved artemisia may fade to green.

THE BEST TIME TO DIVIDE PERENNIALS

Know your plants' needs and heritage. More is not always best. The best time to divide perennials — or shrubs, for that matter — is when they're not in bloom. When a plant is blooming, all its energy is devoted to the effort. That's not the time to shock it with division and the challenge of new root growth. For best results, divide midsummer- to fall-blooming perennials in early spring; divide spring- and early-blooming perennials in late summer or early fall. But remember that dividing plants is like pruning. The time to do it is when you can get around to it. It's better to do it anytime than not to do it at all.

Don't try to raise more plants than you have room for, or strength and time to cultivate. A few plants well cared for are better than a neglected garden — a most discouraging sight.

Don't try to follow all the advice that is offered you; make up your own mind what you want to do and go steadily ahead. If you fail you will know how, and why, which is in itself a distinct gain. Distrust garrulous advice; the gardener with real knowledge is not inclined to force advice upon others.

— Ida Bennett, *The Flower Garden,* 1903

Our Favorite Perennials &
Our Advice for Growing Them

Aster *Aster novae-angliae*

We love to recall that our hardy native New England aster has been grown and treasured by British gardeners since the early 17th century, when the noted plant explorer John Tradescant, Jr., carried these wild daisies home. Let us make every effort to spare these lovely flowers, known in England as Michaelmas daisies, from the fate of the prophet without honor in his homeland.

Asters, which wandered into our gardens from field and roadside, are the glory of fall. As their lineage suggests, they need very little coddling to succeed and come through all but the most severe winters unharmed.

❦ In deep, rich soils, New England asters may grow as tall as eight feet and bear heads of blossoms in shades of lavender and purple with a bright yellow center.

❦ To avoid staking them and to increase flowering, cut the plant down by one-half in June.

❦ Every three to four years, divide large clumps in either spring or fall.

Astilbe *Astilbe* x *arendsii*

Astilbes are among the easiest-to-grow and most colorful shade-tolerant perennials, and they are underappreciated as candidates for cutting. Earlier in this century, astilbes were often forced for houseplants, especially at Easter. Their feathery plumes in white or pink are distinctive and unusual, and their finely cut foliage is dark green or bronze. We especially like 'Peach Blossom', an old-fashioned cultivar that is deliciously fragrant and sports reddish foliage.

❦ Leave the seed heads on the plant after the bloom has passed, unless you find them unattractive.

❦ Astilbes like moist, rich, slightly acid soil. They're heavy feeders and benefit from annual fertilization.

> *Some time when you are weary of the vagaries of*
> *columbine or the infections of delphinium, plant a lot of*
> *astilbes and enjoy a few seasons of utter peace.*
> — Helen Van Pelt Wilson,
> *The New Perennials Preferred,* 1953

Baby's Breath *Gypsophila elegans*

Baby's breath is a hardy perennial with fabulous clouds of small, starry white flowers. Fresh or dried, baby's breath is a mainstay for airy bouquets.

- ❦ Take cuttings of the plant in spring or summer. (The double variety doesn't grow reliably from seed.)
- ❦ Give it full sun and well-drained soil, and settle it into place; it resents being moved.
- ❦ For best results, give gypsophila lime in the spring. It must have an alkaline soil, as its etymology suggests: *gypsos* (gypsum, or lime) and *philos* (loving).
- ❦ Baby's breath is a good candidate for a grow-through support; it practically smothers its own leaves in masses of flowers.
- ❦ Deadhead the plants for repeat bloom in late summer.
- ❦ To use in dried bouquets, harvest the flowers when they are past the bud stage but have not fully opened. Air-dry.

Bee Balm *Monarda didyma*

Spectacular, long-blooming bee balm, also known as Oswego tea, is a charming wildflower we've taken into our gardens and become very fond of growing. As one of its names suggests, it can be brewed into a minty tea and has many medicinal properties. It doesn't attract bees, however, although its brilliant red blossoms are highly attractive to hummingbirds. Borne on stalks two to four feet high, the flowers are wide-mouthed and very fragrant.

- ❦ Bee balm prefers moist, slightly acid soil, but it will grow nearly anywhere, even occasionally becoming too much of a good thing.

❦ Grow it some distance from other plants, in gorgeous masses, especially against a dark background.

Bellflower *Campanula medium*

Nearly all the bellflowers are blue, with drooping, bell-shaped blossoms that make an inimitable contribution to the richness of a garden. *C. medium,* the hardy biennial called Canterbury bells, is a cottage garden classic that was grown in colonial dooryard gardens, evoking memories of cathedral fields and ringing bells.

❦ Canterbury bells can be grown in sun or partial shade in well-drained garden soil.

❦ When grown from seed, they do not flower their first year. Sow seeds one-eighth inch deep, digging in a little manure or bone meal, and thin seedlings to about a foot apart, keeping them in a shady spot. In their second year, the compact rosettes elongate to a radiating mass of stems, and they stretch to splendid bloom from early June to mid-July.

❦ Canterbury bells sprawl a bit but do well planted among stronger, leafy perennials and don't usually need staking.

❦ By promptly removing the flower stalks after the first flush of bloom, you can encourage a second flowering.

❦ Divide plants in spring or fall.

Black-eyed Susan *Rudbeckia fulgida*

Black- or brown-eyed, this sunny daisy-like plant is one of the easiest to grow. Once established, it's drought hardy and provides strong garden color from July to September and plenty of flowers for cutting.

❦ Rudbeckia likes full sun.

❦ Plant it in moist or moderately well drained soil.

❦ It may be divided frequently.

❦ Don't deadhead it if you like the seed heads.

❦ Tall varieties, such as *R. nitida,* need staking.

Bleeding Heart *Dicentra spectabilis*

Although old-fashioned bleeding heart has a native cousin, it is the Chinese species that is most widely cultivated and most familiar. By the turn of the century, it was already regarded as

old-fashioned; the flower was immensely popular in Victorian times, when it was often used in decorative patterns for wallpaper, textiles, and embroidery. Energetic Robert Fortune, one of the most successful plant hunters in history, brought a bleeding heart home to London from the Far East in 1846, and it was an immediate success.

Under optimum conditions (moist soil and partial shade), clumps of bleeding heart can attain remarkable size and dramatic presence, as its Latin name suggests. In late spring, its arching stems bow toward the ground, laden with dangling dark pink hearts, all perfectly shaped and of fascinating construction. Each flower presents two pairs of flower petals: one outer, forming the heart; one inner, forming the "drop of blood" as the heart opens to reveal the stamens. In the right spot, bleeding heart is long-lived and survives neglect, always rising again in the spring to begin another spectacular cycle of growth.

❦ Bleeding heart thrives in a shady, open spot.

❦ It prefers rich, moist soil.

❦ Roots can be divided in spring, or the plant can be propagated by taking root cuttings in early summer.

❦ Grown from seed, it should be sown in flats in mid-summer.

❦ During the summer, its leaves die back, so it is best planted with annuals such as nicotiana or with foxgloves, which will grow up to cover the dying foliage.

❦ Remove yellowing foliage in late summer when it becomes unsightly.

Chrysanthemum *Chrysanthemum* spp.

In the Victorian language of flowers, chrysanthemums stand for optimism and cheerfulness. It's a message easy to read in their exuberant bloom and dazzling variety.

By "chrysanthemums," most of us mean hardy garden mums, whose range in shape and size is outdone only by their range in color. Garden chrysanthemums, once officially *C.* × *morifolium,* have been renamed *Dendranthema* × *grandiflora* but are still best known as chrysanthemums. Most varieties are perennial to at least Zone 5 and grow to three feet or

more, with strong stalks good for cutting and such a profusion of bloom that the flowers may completely hide
the foliage.

Pinch a leaf: chrysanthemums' distinctively sturdy but
lacy foliage has a sharp, spicy aroma. We love them for their
shapely symmetry and their long life in both bouquets and
borders and because they're easy to grow. Potted fall chrysanthemums provide instant color whether you plant them as
part of a landscape scheme, pop them into blanks in a border,
or arrange them in containers. It's so easy to use potted
chrysanthemums for instant effect that many of us may overlook their potential as landscape perennials.

There are thousands of cultivars within the category of
hardy chrysanthemums, and choosing those with different
blooming periods can give you flowers from late summer
well into fall, even past several frosts. New cultivars are developed every year, so a reliable grower is your best guide to the
habits and hardiness of a particular plant.

❦ Chrysanthemums are so accommodating that they can be
   transplanted in bloom.

❦ To grow perennial chrysanthemums, be sure to buy hardy
   chrysanthemums, not florist's chrysanthemums, which
   can't tolerate winter's cycles of freezing and thawing.

❦ How can you tell if you have a winter-hardy mum? These
   mums form a rosette of leaves at their crown when they
   finish blooming. If you don't see the basal rosette, don't
   bother setting it in the garden.

❦ Chrysanthemums can be planted in either spring or fall,
   as long as the roots have a chance to develop before the
   ground freezes. (If you garden in a colder zone, spring
   planting may be safer.) Don't plant shallow-rooted
   chrysanthemums more than 2½ to 3 inches deep.

❦ Wherever they grow, for best results they need full sun (at
   least five hours a day) and light or sandy, well-drained
   soil amended with humus and cow manure or a balanced
   fertilizer.

❦ Chrysanthemums are heavy feeders, so fertilize them
   biweekly until the buds begin to show color.

❦ If you have a heavy, clay soil, amend it with sand or gravel and keep the young plants as high as possible so that they won't get wet feet. Also, if your soil is heavy or your winters are cold, dig up your chrysanthemums in fall and move them to a protected spot. Mulch lightly with coarse straw, corn shocks, or evergreen boughs. In spring, move them back to the garden.

❦ For wintering over, plant chrysanthemums in a relatively sheltered, well-drained spot out of cold, dry winds. Or winter them over in containers kept barely moist in an unheated garage. It's not the cold but the wetness that kills chrysanthemums; they rot.

❦ Raised beds are another alternative for wintering over. Keep soil moist at first, to promote fall root growth, then mulch when temperatures drop.

❦ For spring planting, start with either seeds or young plants grown from cuttings, available at garden centers or through mail-order catalogs. Plant them after the last frost through mid-July.

❦ Pinch them back during spring and summer to promote branching and dense bloom. They'll be ready for their first pinch a few weeks after you plant them, as soon as their new shoots are three to four inches long, and should be pinched until about a month before you want them to start blooming. In the North, that usually means about mid-July; in the South, keep pinching until late July or even mid-August for late bloomers.

❦ Wait until spring to cut back established chrysanthemums, so that their leaves will protect the tender crown. When grown this way, chrysanthemums grow taller and become more open in habit, with longer sprays of blossoms, especially after a few years in the garden.

❦ Garden chrysanthemums are photoperiodic, which means they need short days and long nights to bloom. Nights of about 12 hours trigger bud formation and flowering, although chrysanthemums differ in this regard. Early bloomers need fewer hours of darkness and start to bloom in late August. In mild climates, chrysanthemums may bloom again in spring, as long winter nights set off their bloom clocks.

❦ Be sure to plant mums at least 20 feet from streetlights or other night lights. Upsetting the normal hours of darkness will throw mums off schedule, and they may not flower.

Columbine *Aquilegia vulgaris*

Columbine, also known as granny's bonnet, has bold red-and-yellow flowers in its native form but springs up in old-fashioned gardens in blue and pink, white and purple, both single and double in form. Take the time to really look at a columbine. Some say the petals look like eagles, some like doves.

The natural hybridization of columbines is legendary. Most species that flower at the same time or similar times hybridize and produce mysterious garden newcomers. Plants range in size from six-inch-tall alpines to grand three-foot-tall hybrids.

❦ Columbine is rated as a short-lived perennial, but once it's established in your garden, new plants will pop up all around and bloom early and over a fairly long season. Shake the black seeds out of the dried heads wherever you'd like a new plant.

❦ Good drainage and slightly acid soil rich in humus are essential for growing columbines.

❦ They do best in light or partial shade but can tolerate full sun except in extremely hot or dry regions.

❦ A light, sandy, moist soil in a sheltered spot is preferable. Many columbines will grow well in semishade, and they are favorites in the rock garden and perennial border.

❦ To germinate, columbine seeds require alternating periods of warmth, cold, and warmth, as in summer, winter, and spring. Germination is best with fresh seeds. Packaged seeds may be disappointing because the deep dormancy can be broken only by mimicking the natural cycle. Seeds are viable for five years or more. Seeds sown in early spring may bloom the first year and will give good bloom the second. Germination may be best at below 65° F and in bright, indirect light. Or start indoors: Sow seeds on top of fine, moistened potting soil in an open container, cover with a plastic bag, and refrigerate for about 4 weeks. Then move the chilled container to a windowsill or other warm, sunny spot. Germination should begin in 14 to 21 days.

🐛 When transplanting, find a more or less permanent location, as columbines don't like to be moved or divided; they develop an extensive root system. Space plants 12 to 18 inches apart.

Coreopsis *Coreopsis* spp.

Bright yellow daisy-like coreopsis, also called tickseed and calliopsis, is easy to confuse with black-eyed Susan but has distinctive, jagged-edged petal tips. Its Latin name comes from its resemblance to bedbugs (the Greek word for bedbug is *koris*) because American pioneers who found it on the Great Plains believed that its seeds would repel bedbugs and ticks. It's an American native and a great garden flower, beloved by beginners and meadow gardeners.

🐛 Don't plant hardy, drought-tolerant coreopsis in rich soil. It has evolved to thrive in lean, sandy soil, and that's what it needs to survive.

🐛 Deadhead for repeat bloom.

Daylily *Hemerocallis* spp.

The modern daylily is a gorgeous hybrid cultivar bred for garden display — not to be confused with the ubiquitous naturalized tawny daylily *(Hemerocallis fulva)*, which is descriptively called homestead lily, roadside lily, and, worse, ditch lily. (Not that there's anything *wrong* with *H. fulva;* it's a beautiful plant.)

All species, or wild, daylilies (including lemon daylilies, *H. lilio-asphodelus*) are native to Asia, where they have a long history in both the garden and the larder. What part of a daylily is not eaten? The tender foliage is eaten as a spring green; the buds are eaten raw and in soups and sauces; the flowers are eaten, steamed or stir-fried, even when spent; the swollen portions of the roots are boiled and eaten. All parts have a mild peppery taste and a thickening effect. Even in early spring, a thicket of fast-growing daylily leaves marks the coming glory of a midsummer garden. Tall, beautiful, deep orange daylilies *(H. fulva)* are prolific in American gardens. The perfect perennials, daylilies are robust, long-lived, rewarding, unfussy, minimal-care plants that are remarkably free from insects and diseases.

❦ Daylilies like good, well-drained soil. They'll survive with little or no watering, but they'll flourish if well watered. If you remember that a daylily blossom is 95 percent water, you'll understand that a budding plant needs a tall draft.

❦ Daylilies can take some shade, but they really require a full six hours of sunshine to achieve their potential; even five hours is not quite enough. They hate deep shade but often won't die, just withhold the glory of their blooms.

❦ The rule for dividing plants has long been to divide clumps every three years. Don't follow this rule strictly; instead, consider the vigor of the plant. Some clump-forming daylilies grow so slowly that they never need dividing; others may be ready to divide in five years, or eight or ten years. Take a good look at a specific clump. As new stems develop above the old crowns, the new plants are hoisted above the soil in a sort of hummock. This is the signal to divide, because the new plants need more access to soil, water, and nutrients.

❦ Be sure to transplant root divisions with their crowns. It is easy to make a mistake if you don't understand how a daylily grows. A daylily has four organs: roots, stem or crown, leaves, and flowers. (The flower-bearing "stem" does not function as a stem and is properly called a scape.) The roots anchor the plant in the soil and take up water and nutrients. The leaves practice photosynthesis, and the flowers are involved in reproduction. The crown, the point at which the leaves and roots meet, is the key junction — that's where all the action is. On a daylily, the stem is compacted, accordion style, so that you can barely see the internodes and buds that will become next year's plants. To form a new plant, you need part of the stem; the root alone won't do it.

Dividing a daylily is easy. Daylilies have shallow root systems. Loosen a clump, lift it up, shake off the dirt, and split it into fans by twisting and pulling, using two spading forks back to back or whatever it takes. Then cut the leaves back to less than a foot, being sure to keep the crown.

🐾 Do not judge a cultivar by flower alone. There's more to a great daylily than the bloom. Experts look for good, spreading scapes branching out to hold buds presentably and a high bud count for continuous flowering. An excellent scape might have 30 to 35 buds, which means the plant will bloom every day for a month. The foliage is another important consideration, as it's visible in the garden far longer than the flower and must be at least presentable. Certain foliage appeals to certain gardeners; be sure to consider it, as well as the relation of the scape to the leaves and the general shape of the plant.

🐾 For good effect, group plants of the same variety rather than scattering different plants. Each cultivar multiplies at its own rate and has a different type of foliage. Even if the differences are subtle, with the passage of time a scattered planting takes on a more and more mixed appearance. In contrast, the visual impact of large masses of one variety is fantastic.

Daylilies are my deepest obsession. They're bright and gorgeous, hard to kill, hard to damage, and if you feed them, they love you. They like a weak solution of Epsom salts and don't mind a fertilizer — either organic or chemical.

— Lucie Wilkins, Woodbridge, Connecticut

Delphinium *Delphinium elatum*
Our modern delphinium, also called candle larkspur, is a mainstay of gardens around the world. Native to China, Siberia, Europe, and North America, hardy *D. elatum* grows to five feet or more, with spectacular spikes of flowers in shades of blue, violet, mauve, and white. The shape of the blossoms has suggested both the botanical and common names for this flower. *Delphinium* is from the Greek for dolphin, for the long spur of the flower resembles the nose of a dolphin. This spur also suggested the common names larkspur, lark's-heel, and lark's-claw.

- Delphiniums prefer full sun or very light shade.
- They do best in a rich, slightly acid soil. They like lots of water, especially just before and during flowering.
- Delphiniums are very hardy in all but the coldest climates; they are more likely to be killed by poor drainage, smothering, or diseases than by low temperatures. It's always a good idea to protect seedlings transplanted in fall from frost heaving. Cover the plants with about two inches of sand and later mulch with salt hay or straw to give the necessary protection. Cover the crowns with ashes to discourage crown rot.
- In the South, the key is planting them in fall and letting them winter over for spring bloom. It's also a good idea to choose a heat-tolerant variety such as *D. grandiflorum* 'Blue Mirror'.
- Fancy "Chinese" delphiniums, blue as the legendary skies of Delphi, in Greece, are tricky to grow in hot climates, but where summers are cool and they are sheltered from wind, they are the most glorious summer flowers. (In warmer regions, grow annual larkspur instead.)
- Cut the flowering stems (but not their leaves) to the ground as soon as possible after they have finished flowering and then fertilize, to encourage new shoots to come up in time to blossom in fall.

Delphiniums [are] an enormous challenge. Their main enemies are fungi and sudden wind and rain. My solutions have been garden sulfur spread in April and kept at the ready all summer — and telescoping stakes to fasten them to as they grow.
I've found that if you take the blooms into the house as soon as they open, the plants will bloom again.

— Joan Withington,
Hillsborough Center, New Hampshire

Feverfew *Chrysanthemum parthenium*

Though not native to America, feverfew has been around as long as the Republic; even longer, in fact, for the Puritans brought it to Massachusetts in the 1600s because of its medicinal properties, and it was listed in a seed catalog as early as 1833. Old-time Appalachian herbalists call it feverfuge, which is very close to its Old English name, *feferfuge,* a corruption of the Latin *febrifugia.* As its name implies, feverfew is a traditional cure for fever, and recent research has suggested that eating the fresh leaves can ease migraines. Few garden plants are as easy to grow and as long blooming as feverfew, which flowers from June until frost.

❦ The more you cut the flowers, the more the plant will produce. To stagger bloom, cut every third stem to half its length in mid-June.

❦ Feverfew self-sows prolifically and produces offsets from clumps. Grown from seed, it flowers the second season and transplants without complaint.

❦ It's drought tolerant, fills in garden gaps, and makes ample bouquets of creamy daisy-like flowers and earthy-scented ferny foliage.

❦ Adaptable feverfew combines well with foxgloves and old roses. Is it any wonder it's an old-fashioned favorite?

[Feverfew is] so cheerful; it blooms forever, fills in all the gaps in the garden, is drought tolerant, and spreads wildly. Feverfew is great for cut flowers: there are as many as 50 individual flower heads per plant, and it lasts in a bouquet until it turns brown — it never drops petals. I don't know many people who grow it. I started mine from seeds my mother sent me from Iowa, but now I have a hedge of it. It's breathtaking.

— Beth Waterman, Big Indian, New York

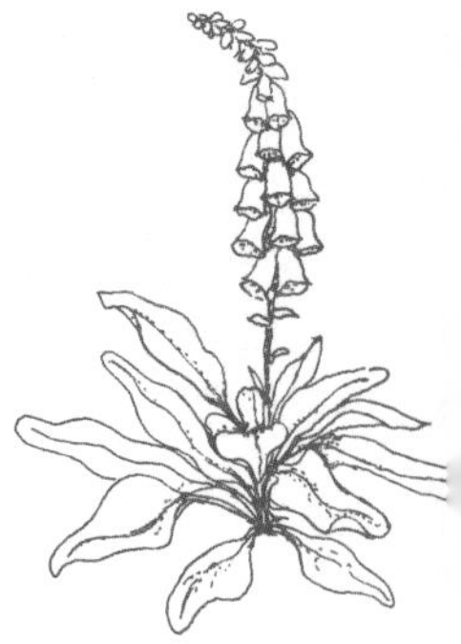

Foxglove *Digitalis purpurea*

Stately foxglove, an English wildflower, has been a garden favorite for centuries. Both English and German settlers brought foxglove seeds to America very early and scattered them on the edges of their homesteads. Foxglove soon escaped from the coastal settlements and began the trek westward, so rapidly that when John Bradbury went into the new land of the Louisiana Purchase in 1809 to collect wildflowers, he found foxgloves wherever pioneers had passed. Interestingly, the presence of foxgloves is an indicator of minerals in the soil, so Russian prospectors search for new iron deposits and coalfields by helicopter, looking for masses of foxgloves.

Foxglove is hardy and designed for traveling. There are 80,000 foxglove seeds to an ounce, and the wind shakes them out of their papery capsules and scatters them lavishly every fall. Large colonies sometimes form in the wild, a stunning sight to see along a road or in a sunny forest clearing.

Foxglove also is a powerful herb and was identified as a potent heart remedy in 1768. (The active chemical in its leaves is called digitalin.) It is native to northern Europe and England, where it has grown wild for centuries and was used by the druids to heal and harm. Today it's raised commercially for medicinal use, and strains that are richer in glycosides (which combine to form its natural healing ingredient) have been developed. In the garden tall, magenta foxglove has an air of mystery, keeping these secrets as it attracts bees and hummingbirds with its heavily spotted masses of bells and providing us with striking and long-lasting flowers.

- Rich in oil, starch, protein, and sugar, the seeds have a high rate of germination and thrive in well-drained, fertile soil, preferring the shadier side of the garden.
- Foxglove is a biennial or perennial. Frequent division in spring helps maintain its perennial character.
- Remove faded flowers but leave some seed heads for reseeding.

Geranium, Hardy *Geranium* spp.
Hardy, or cranesbill, geraniums are versatile, indispensable, and easy to grow. They're native to England and Europe — in great variety — and no relation at all to the tender pelargoniums we commonly call geraniums (see Chapter 2). They're known as cranesbill because of the narrow, beaklike structure at the top of their fruit.

- ❦ Geraniums flourish in full sun or partial shade, although exposure to prolonged heat slows their blooming.
- ❦ They do fine in almost any soil, filling out the border or rock garden, working as a ground cover or among shrubs and roses.
- ❦ Some of the best cultivars are 'Johnson's Blue' and 'Wargrave Pink'.
- ❦ To keep them bright, deadhead after blooming or shear to the ground.
- ❦ Divide crowded plants and propagate by division in spring or fall.

Goldenrod *Solidago canadensis*
Goldenrod flowers with profuse abandon. Naturalized throughout England and Japan, our gorgeous native goldenrod has yet to gain the acceptance it deserves in American gardens. Perhaps it's because of the mistaken idea that it causes hay fever — or is it just too close to home to seem as exotic as it looks?

- ❦ Goldenrod is extremely hardy and easy to grow from seed. Sow it outdoors in fall.
- ❦ *S. canadensis* has big, splashy blossoms and stays golden for up to two months.
- ❦ Goldenrod spreads by rhizomes (swollen underground stems). If it threatens to take over the garden, prune the rhizomes in fall with a sharp spade.

Hollyhock *Alcea rosea*
No flowers are more characteristic of an old-fashioned garden than hollyhocks, which are most charming growing in clumps at the back of the border or near a rustic fence. Nostalgic gardeners prefer the classic single varieties.

Hollyhocks were grown in ancient China both as ornamental plants and for food. Country folk ate the leaves, cooked like other spring greens, and the flower buds, which were considered a delicacy. Hollyhocks are native to the Near East and were carried home to Europe by the Crusaders. (Their name dates from this connection. They were called "holy" because they grew so profusely in the Holy Land and "hock" like other members of the mallow family.) Hollyhocks have been common in British gardens since the 15th century, standing beside old walls and cottage doors. By 1650, there were dozens of named varieties, both single and double, in a wide range of colors, from white, pink, cream, and yellow to red, maroon, and salmon.

Carried to North America by 1631, hollyhocks settled in and took off, spreading so fast despite neglect that they were sometimes called "alley orchids." Thomas Jefferson raised hollyhocks at Monticello and favored one Old World variety, 'Nigra', with single, dark (almost black) blossoms.

🌱 Hollyhocks thrive in almost any soil as long as they get plenty of sun.

🌱 Most are biennials and bloom their second summer, but a planting of them is likely to be perennial in character as it renews itself through self-seeding. Sow seeds for next year's flowers or set out hollyhock plants two feet apart in early spring.

🌱 The hollyhock's seedpods, which look like tiny wheels of cheese, are edible. One recipe calls for sautéeing them in oil and adding them to salads. "Cheeses" is an old-fashioned name for these pods.

I suppose I'm in love with hollyhocks partly because my mother forbade me to plant them. My mother believed they'd attract Japanese beetles. She wouldn't have them in the garden. Now I grow them, and they're all the more delicious for being forbidden. They're one of the joys of my life.

— Rebecca Owen, Saluda, Virginia

Hosta *Hosta* spp.

Hostas are members of the lily family and were formerly called plantain lilies and funkias. They are grown primarily for their foliage, although most varieties have small flowers on wands in mid- to late summer. Our favorite is *H. plantaginea* 'Aphrodite', which has very fragrant double white flowers.

Hostas offer a tremendous variety of leaf shape, size, form, and color. Although most are green, some are golden and some variegated. Some leaves are giant and puckered, others quilted or ridged. Some people grow hundreds of varieties, but that's only a small portion of the 1,200 cultivars available in this country.

❦ One of the most undemanding plants you can grow, hostas prefer acid soil and thrive in dappled shade.

❦ They will grow in dry areas, windswept places, or under a high canopy of trees. They can go for long periods without much water, although they do better (like most plants) with a regular supply of moisture. It's easier to keep the soil around a hosta plant moist if you mulch it.

❦ Before you plant a hosta, improve the soil with manure and compost; additional feeding won't be necessary.

❦ Hostas are easily divided in spring or fall. If only one more plant is needed, simply dig it from the edge of an existing clump. To make several divisions, lift the entire clump and pull apart the fleshy roots by hand; or score them with a knife, making sure that each division has at least one large bud.

There is no real need ever to separate hostas. They can stay in the same spot forever. Some grow to four feet high and seven feet wide. They spread laterally and send out lateral shoots. You never see one mature plant with babies next to it.

— Bob Seawright, Carlisle, Massachusetts

Iris *Iris* spp.

Tall, beautiful iris, named after the Greek goddess of the rainbow, comes in all the rainbow's colors except pure red. Heirloom and old-fashioned irises are especially charming. One of the best varieties is pale blue *I. pallida,* which some gardeners plant just for its foliage, especially in its variegated forms. Most familiar to gardeners are the tall (at least 28 inches and sometimes nearly twice that) bearded irises *(I. germanica).* These hybrids are descended from the European-Mediterranean gene pool and show off the ingenuity of American iris breeders — not only with their amazing colors but also in ruffles and frills, velvety trim, and wonderful fragrance, which ranges from sweet to spicy, musky to lemony. Antique irises tend to be smaller than their bearded cousins, but they're hardy, pest free, and often fragrant. Some of the best varieties are 'Florentina', 'Honorabile', and 'Madame Chareau'. Reblooming irises also are quite hardy and provide a bloom in the spring and again in the fall. They come in all types, sizes, and colors.

Iris cultivation dates to ancient times but was popular in Europe by the Middle Ages. The fleur-de-lis adorns the French royal standard and is the symbol of Florence, Italy. American native species irises awaited early settlers, who also imported Old World varieties to use as herbal medicines. Orrisroot, taken from the dried roots of *I. germanica* 'Florentina', was used to cure blood and lung diseases.

❧ Match the iris to the environment. Irises suited to almost every habitat are available.

❧ The bigger the rhizome, the better the bloom.

❧ Give irises at least half a day of sun and well-drained soil. If they don't get enough sun, they won't bloom.

❧ Unlike bulbs, which thrive deep underground, iris rhizomes (thickened stems that grow horizontally) need sun and air to dry them out after a rainfall. If they're covered with soil or crowded with other plants, they'll rot. Only the roots, which dangle off the rhizomes, should go underground.

❦ If your soil is very acid, sweeten it with a bit of lime.

❦ Don't trim iris leaves into a fan. Leaves carry on photosynthesis and develop nourishment for next year's growth. Cut off brown tips if you must, and cut the flower stalk down to the rhizome to discourage rot.

❦ When iris rhizomes multiply and get crowded, their blossoms get smaller and smaller. For big, healthy blooms, dig up the rhizomes, divide them, and replant them every three or four years. The best time to do it is right after they've bloomed. That's the usual time to plant irises, too — in mid- to late summer — and that's when you'll find them in local nurseries. To divide irises, cut off any rot and the oldest, central part of the rhizome (which has no leaves). Divide it into a single fan or a Y-shaped double fan with a set of leaves (about two to six inches of rhizome and some roots). Dangle the long, stringy roots into a deep hole, then fill with soil and compost and pack firmly. You may want to make a ridge or a little mound of soil so that the rhizome has a perch for basking in the sun.

❦ Good companions for irises are self-sowing annuals such as love-in-a-mist, silvery lamb's ears, blue flax flowers, small poppies, and catmint, which will grow happily alongside irises and fill in when their blooming season is over.

Lady's-mantle *Alchemilla mollis*

Lady's-mantle's distinctive scalloped gray-green leaves collect rain and dew, which shine in silvery beads gathered by hopeful alchemists during the Middle Ages, hence its Latin name. Modern gardeners have their own reasons for loving this plant. Native to Europe, Asia, and Greenland, low-growing lady's-mantle is hardy, shade loving, and perennially evergreen. It's tumbling chartreuse flowers bloom from late spring to early summer and are wonderful in bouquets, fresh or dried.

❦ Lady's-mantle makes a wonderful carpet under roses.

❦ It does well in poor, dry soils and doesn't mind a bit of shade.

❦ Lady's-mantle may self-sow. In spring, move the new seedlings to make a lovely garden edging.

❦ By midsummer, the velvety ruffled leaves may look a bit tattered. Then it's time to shear them to the ground, remove any tired foliage, and wait for fresh growth.

Lavender *Lavandula* spp.

Fragrant, perennial lavender, native to the Mediterranean region, is hardy in most parts of the country and beloved wherever it grows. The flowers have a sharp, refreshing fragrance, and the scent of the narrow, linear leaves is reminiscent of mixed spices and turpentine. Dried, lavender makes a pretty sachet, and it has many medicinal uses.

❦ Give lavender strong sun and excellent drainage.

❦ In a site with dry winters and hot summers, it can become a hedge.

❦ Mulch it well in cold-weather climates and cut it back hard (to about three inches) in spring.

❦ The 30 species of lavender vary a good deal in size, foliage, flower color, and hardiness, so experiment a bit to find one that will work in your garden.

❦ If you shear plants back by one-third after they bloom, they will rebloom.

❦ To propagate, rip (don't clip) two- to three-inch cuttings from the side shoots. Tear the cutting downward, taking a piece of the older wood with it. Set it in moist, sandy soil.

Lenten Rose *Helleborus orientalis*

Hellebores are miraculous. Any plant that blooms in winter is to be treasured, but these elegant, free-blooming, superhardy "roses" also are easy to grow. They stay evergreen all year unless you have a deep, persistent snow cover, and they produce elegant, nodding flowers in a range of pinks and whites.

❦ Give Lenten rose partial shade and rich, moist, well-drained soil.

❦ In early spring, just before bloom, remove the old foliage.

❦ Top-dress hellebores with well-rotted manure to keep soil fertility high, and they will happily self-seed and increase in size, even becoming a handsome ground cover.

Lupine *Lupinus polyphyllus*

Hardy, perennial lupines put on a great show in cool climates, spreading to fill whole fields in some places. Wild lupines thrive on roadsides and barren slopes, preferring disturbed areas where nothing else will grow. Once they settle into an appropriate spot, they will grow there indefinitely, self-sowing and providing year-round interest with their spiky blossoms, attractive leaves, and interesting seedpods.

❦ Lupines prefer barren, sandy slopes, light soil, and full sun.

❦ The neon-bright Russell hybrids like a richer soil.

❦ Transplant lupines when they're dormant, or sow seeds outdoors in fall, nicking them first.

Penstemon *Penstemon* spp.

Perennial penstemons all descend from a vast genus of North American native flowers and range from diminutive alpines to tough desert plants. Sometimes called beardtongue, penstemon gets this name because of the tiny hairs that develop on the lower lip of the tubular flowers. In the American West, it's also called deadman's bells, for naturalizing in graveyards. Despite these unflattering names, penstemon is one of the loveliest plants, beloved for its use in water-thrifty gardens.

Most penstemons have attractive foliage and showy, snapdragon-like flowers in a wide variety of colors. A great many species are cultivated, and they are among the hardiest of our garden plants. Pine-leaf penstemon *(Penstemon pinifolius)* and Rocky Mountain penstemon *(Penstemon strictus)* are two species of native penstemon. Pine-leaf penstemon grows 12 to 15 inches tall and has narrow red flowers. It was named for its needlelike dark green foliage. Rocky Mountain penstemon has flowers that range from royal blue to purple. Its deep green foliage is grasslike at the top and broad and lance-shaped at the bottom. Both of these penstemons are hardy in Zones 4 or 5 to 9.

❦ Penstemons are tolerant of poor or dry soils, heat, and full sun. They do appreciate some shade in hot climates.

❦ They require good drainage, as a wet soil rots their roots and invites problems.

- Penstemons require light to germinate, often self-sow readily, and can benefit from a light mulch in winter.
- In colder zones, take cuttings in early fall for over-wintering.
- Remove faded flower stalks to prolong bloom. Divide plants in spring as needed.

Peony *Paeonia* spp.

After at least 2,000 years of cultivation and breeding in China, the peony was introduced to Europe and America in about 1800. It was love at first sight, and that love has lasted. Sixty or 70 years ago, catalogs listed only three types of peonies — white, crimson, and rose pink; today thousands of varieties are available.

Peonies are easy to grow and remarkably hardy, have lovely foliage, stand straight and tall (with maybe a grow-through ring or a bit of staking), and make magnificent cut flowers. They may be the longest-lived flowers; individual plants have been known to live a century. Get them settled in the garden, and you can leave them to your grandchildren. Even when they're not in bloom, they're handsome.

- Since peonies are nigh immortal, it makes sense to start them out right. Dig a good hole (at least 18 inches deep) and fill it with enriched soil, then set the peony near the surface, covering the crowns or growing tips with only 1½ inches of soil.
- Peonies must have excellent drainage. Give them shelter from wind and prepare to stake them when they get top-heavy.
- After planting or moving, peonies take time to settle in, but they're forgiving. Be patient; it usually takes about three years to produce a full crop of blossoms.
- After blooming, deadhead to the first strong leaf. In fall, cut the foliage to the ground to avoid any overwintering diseases.
- Don't get out the spray if you see ants on your peony buds. They're supping on sweet nectar and offer protection against all bud-eating pests in return.

Phlox, Garden *Phlox paniculata*

Phlox has been cultivated for centuries. One of the reasons it's so well adapted to our gardens is that it's an American native — both the perennial form *(P. paniculata)*, which originated in the South, and the annual *(P. drummondii,* Drummond's phlox or Texas pride; see page 47). Of the 60 to 70 species currently recognized, all but one are native to the Americas.

The phlox family includes some of the most widely grown garden favorites. Characteristically, the blossoms have a very short tube and five lobes so that the flower appears to have five separate petals. The flowers are usually sweet smelling and conjure up memories of a Victorian country garden.

❦ Set out new plants in either fall or early spring, or sow seeds one-quarter inch deep in full sun as soon as the trees leaf out.

❦ Phlox love even moisture and resent transplanting. Handle seedlings very carefully.

❦ Most phlox require a slightly acid, moist, loamy soil amended with generous amounts of humus.

❦ Powdery mildew sometimes afflicts phlox, so choose mildew-resistant varieties or, as garden guru Elsa Bakalar says, "pretend you like it." To help prevent mildew, keep plants a couple of feet apart and take out about a third of the total stems to allow for good air circulation (and stronger bloom). Cut down stalks in fall so that mildew won't winter over. Most of the time, spraying is ineffective.

❦ Divide clumps of perennial phlox every three years to keep them vigorous. Cut back the plant by one-third after it flowers, then dig up and divide.

❦ Many phlox self-sow and cultivars may revert to species magenta. To prevent this, deadhead rigorously. Pinch back weaker stems to prolong flowering; this encourages branching and gives another flush of flowers.

❦ Cut phlox for bouquets; it's long lasting and sweet scented.

- The stalks you leave in the garden will attract moths and butterflies all day long and evening moths as the sun goes down.
- Perennial blue phlox *(P. divaricata)*, sometimes known as wild sweet William, which grows wild in many parts of the South, is most at home in a semishady woodland. Keep this in mind when you plant this great spring-blooming perennial. Full sun is not ideal for this plant; it will attain its full form only in shade and may bloom for a month.

Pink *Dianthus* spp.

Pinks were grown by monks as long ago as the 13th century and are a staple of the English cottage garden. The early 19th century was the golden age of the pink, and plantsman's lists show a choice of up to 192 varieties. Recently, there has been a revival of interest in some of these beautiful, old varieties, especially the "laced" and patterned ones.

The genus *Dianthus,* which includes the carnation, also includes China pinks, grass pinks, sweet William, and hybrids, some of which are annuals, some biennials, and some hardy perennials. The name *pink* alludes to the pinked or scalloped petal edges, not to the color, which came later. All the members of the pink family have opposite, toothless leaves and swollen joints. Except in their double forms, all have five petals, which are often notched, tattered, or fringed.

- Nearly all pinks like a sunny spot, good drainage, and a reasonably alkaline soil, but maiden pinks *(D. deltoides)* thrive even in partial shade. Pinks do best when sown in autumn.
- Stems on hybrid pinks are stronger today, and there's a fashion for growing long-flowering, low-growing perennial types in the rock garden or front of the border. Many of them have a spicy scent and are hardy.
- Most pinks thrive in Zones 4 to 7; some favor warmer or colder climates. An alpine form, *D. alpinus,* will bloom in Zone 2, and China pinks *(D. chinensis)* are long-season bloomers in Zone 10.
- Pheasant's-eye pinks, also called cottage pinks or grass

pinks, have small, clove-scented flowers, often fringed or feathered, in shades of rose, lavender, and white. This pink, *D. plumarius*, is long-lived and a good cut flower
❧ Superb pinks (*D. superbus*), introduced into gardens as early as 1772, have delicate, feathery lilac flowers with a delicious scent that is particularly noticeable in the morning. The buds are washed with red-lavender, and the foliage is gray-green. They bloom in late spring.

Poppy, Oriental *Papaver orientale*
During its season of bloom, the flamboyant Oriental poppy dominates the garden, amazing us with its intense scarlet color; huge bowl-shaped blossoms (up to 12 inches across); and silky petals, which are sometimes semitransparent, sometimes delicately fringed. The papery petals meet in a blotchy black center with long stamens. Newer colors include pale salmon-pink, dusky gray-pink, and pure white. This long-lived poppy blooms during late spring and early summer. It's easy to grow, even in heavy or clay soil.
❧ Poppies dislike hot, humid climates. They do best in cool climates and in well-drained, alkaline soil that is not too rich. They thrive in full sun.
❧ Keep them picked to stimulate further flowering.
❧ Set out plants in early spring or sow seeds in late spring for bloom in late summer or early fall.

> *I know of no flower that has so many charming tricks and manners, none with a method of growth more picturesque and fascinating. The [poppy's] stalks often take a curve, a twist from some current of air or some impediment, and the fine stems will turn and bend in all sorts of graceful ways, but the bud is always held erect when the time comes for it to blossom.*
>
> — Celia Thaxter, *An Island Garden*, 1894

Rose *Rosa* spp.

In fashionable gardening circles, old-fashioned roses are as hot as meadow gardens, and for the same good reasons. By "old roses" we mean varieties that look and behave like ancestral roses, as opposed to modern roses such as hybrid teas and floribundas. A subset of old rose lovers grow only rugosas, an extremely hardy, freely naturalizing group descended from the species *R. rugosa*. Rugosas are the roses our grandmothers grew, with feathery foliage, large hips, and nostalgic charm.

Most old roses are hardy, vigorous, and extremely varied in shape and color. They are likely to be large, thorny plants with fragrant flowers. Old-fashioned roses combine the strength, variety, and beauty of the old roses with modern traits such as repeat bloom and disease resistance.

🌑 In the end, roses want what all growing things want: to go to seed and increase their own kind. This is where deadheading comes in. Rose growers deadhead religiously. When we first met New York rosarian Michael Ruggiero, he was ruthlessly deadheading a full hedge of glorious yellow roses. "There's a growth bud with every leaf," Ruggiero told us, "so cutting off the fading rose takes the strength that would be going into making seeds and lets the plant make more flowers." Even if the rose is not a rebloomer, cutting spent blossoms about a quarter of an inch above the first leaf with five leaflets saves the plant from expending energy in seed production — in other words, foils its life goal.

🌑 All roses need at least five hours of good sun; six is better, seven better yet. Roses grown in weak sun may not die at once, but they will weaken gradually. In ten years, you'll lose the plant.

🌑 They need water and nourishing soil, especially water.

🌑 Roses dislike any compaction of their roots and wet feet caused by bad drainage. Don't dance around rosebushes; their root systems can't take it. The worst mistake rose growers make is failing to provide good drainage.

🌑 Climbing roses don't climb; they just grow taller and taller, faster and faster. No rose can climb by itself; it has to be tied or trained against a support. Then they take hold and may support the support when they get established. Gertrude Jekyll told us that the great virtue of climbing roses is the way they fall down, cascading from tree and bank and wall.

Roses love water, but they don't like it. That is, they don't like to sit in it (except for Rosa palustris, *the swamp rose). They die if the soil's too wet in winter. Roses like rich, loose soil that drains extremely well. We give them a three-foot soil. The whole trick is in good soil and good drainage. We give each bed two inches [of water] a week; we flood the beds, and in 20 minutes it's gone. That's drainage.*

— Michael Ruggiero, New York Botanical Garden, New York, New York

Veronica *Veronica* spp.

The heirloom veronica, commonly known as speedwell, with its small lilac-blue flowers, is charming and has seen a lot of history. A European native, it arrived on these shores with the earliest settlers. (Remember the *Mayflower*'s sister ship, the *Speedwell*?) It was valued as a medicinal herb and was handed to travelers with the wish, "Speed well." Veronica is sold today in more refined forms and appears in pink and white, as well as blue, versions. It is a profuse bloomer, a good cut flower, and easy to grow.

🌱 Veronica thrives in a bright, sunny spot.

🌱 It tends to collapse, so give it some support (ideally, a grow-through ring). Shear it before it blooms in mid-June for stockier growth.

🌱 If you deadhead the first spikes, it will develop side growth.

Violet *Viola* spp.

Violets have been popular for centuries but were taken up with such great interest by Victorians that they seem expressive of that period. At Windsor Castle, three thousand plants were grown under glass frames to supply the royal household with bunches of fresh flowers through the winter. In the 19th and early 20th centuries, baskets of violets for sale were a common sight on city streets, each little posy encircled with violet or ivy leaves and tied with thread. London clerks often wore a bunch of violets as a boutonniere. Although there was a thriving British industry growing sweet violets, it could never compare to that of the south of France, where some 13,000 pounds of violets were harvested each year for the flower trade.

The violet family, found throughout the temperate regions of the world, includes the violet and the pansy. All are low-growing plants, some producing runners. Violets have basal leaves, either oval or heart-shaped and sometimes cut into fingerlike lobes. The leaves are slightly wrinkled, the stalks grooved, and the margins slightly toothed. The flowers, often highly fragrant, are sometimes nodding and come in violet, blue, reddish purple, lilac, yellow, and white. They have five petals, four arranged in pairs, with the lower petals spurred.

The florist's violet (*V. odorata*), also known as sweet violet, is a tufted perennial native to Europe, Africa, and Asia. *V. canadensis* is hardy in the eastern United States and grows to a foot or more. The sweet white violet (*V. blanda*) has solitary white flowers.

❦ Violets are easily cultivated, but for best results they should have partial shade (as under a tree) and rich, moist soil.

❦ They are propagated by seed, division, or cuttings, and they spread easily. They are never "shrinking" when it comes to taking over new territory.

❦ Violets are heavy feeders and thrive on fertilization.

❦ Pick violets frequently to keep them flowering and prevent them from going to seed.

Yarrow *Achillea* spp.

Yarrow, a hardy perennial, is also a white wildflower. The Chippewas called it squirreltail, which aptly describes its feathery foliage, and it also has been called woundwort and nosebleed for its ability to stop bleeding. It's been smoked, brewed into a tea, and used as snuff (it was once called old-man's-pepper, for its pungent leaves).

Sun-loving yarrow spreads by underground runners and can be a pest in a meadow, for cows hungry enough to eat it will produce milk with an off flavor. It is extremely tough, growing on roadsides and in poor soil, often preventing erosion.

In the garden, given regular care, yarrow, especially in its old-fashioned double variety (*A. ptarmica* 'The Pearl'), may surprise you with its long-blooming, dependable beauty. There is an old superstition that if one sleeps on a bunch of 'The Pearl' on Midsummer Eve, he or she will dream of a future spouse.

❦ Flower heads on some cultivars spread up to five inches across and come in yellow, apricot, red, russet, pink, and beige.

❦ Keep yarrow picked, and deadhead after it blooms if it looks untidy. The foliage may be cut to the ground to encourage regrowth. It may require light staking with bamboo.

❦ Bright yarrow is one of the best flowers for drying. Harvest when the flowers are fully open and terminal clusters are still firm. Do not remove the foliage.

Yucca *Yucca filamentosa*

An elegant desert plant that thrives in most parts of the country, yucca, sometimes called Adam's-needle or bear grass, grows 6 to 8 feet, and sometimes up to 15 feet, tall. It's a staple in old-fashioned gardens and sometimes stands sentinel near an abandoned cellar hole. Its waxy, white orchidlike flowers are edible raw, in salads. Its leaves are swordlike, evergreen, and edged with distinctive curly threads.

❦ Yuccas are very long-lived, hardy, and drought resistant.

❦ Keep their location as desertlike as possible: full sun and well-drained, sandy soil.

❦ Yuccas are easily grown from seed, but they may straggle. Some plants will come up in two to three weeks, some next year.

❦ Cold treatment — placing seeds in the refrigerator a few weeks before sowing — improves germination.

Chapter 4

Sensational Flowering Bulbs

I walk down the garden paths,
And all the daffodils
Are blowing, and the bright blue squills.

— AMY LOWELL (1874–1925)

Daffodil
(*Narcissus* spp.)

*B*ULBS ARE ONE OF THE MOST RELIABLE, MOST VERSATILE groups of plants. Since bulbs are self-packaged growing systems, they are vastly easier to grow than almost any other plant. Busy gardeners delight in them, and thrifty ones value them keenly, for once planted, most of them grow without further care or feeding, some returning year after year. Even experienced gardeners may marvel at the unassuming drabness of spring-blooming bulbs in fall, knowing that they will rise from the cold earth and burst into flower after a season's sleep beneath the snow.

There are bulbs for all seasons and all situations, adaptable to the most formal gardens and for naturalizing, and every gardener can find some reason to grow bulbs in containers, whether indoors or out. In a world where city life and civilization threaten to unseat nature and blur the rotation of the seasons, bulbs provide a reassuring reminder of the enduring patterns of life. We give them light, water, and soil. They give use a splendid succession of color and fragrance from spring to fall.

What Is a Bulb?

We have chosen a broad definition of the word *bulb* to include all plants that form swollen, underground storage roots or stems to carry them through dry or cold seasons. This includes bulbs, corms, tubers, and rhizomes, the victims of an unlikely movement to call storehouse-type plants "geophytes." Strictly speaking, a bulb — the onion is a good example — is made up of the swollen, fleshy bases of leaves. Other storage structures are formed by different parts of the plant; a crocus's corm, for instance, is a swollen stem base. Some irises have both bulbs and tuberous roots; others have rhizomes and fleshy storage roots.

Bulb Planting Basics

❦ Nature never intended for bulbs to loll about aboveground, so don't delay planting them.

❦ To deter mice and moles, put holly, thorny twigs, or leaves in the planting holes. Some gardeners use kitty litter or crushed gravel. If ravenous rodents are a real problem in your garden, you may need to take stronger measures, such as planting bulbs in a cage of wire or a bottomless flowerpot.

❦ Plant all bulbs in well-drained soil. Wet soil leads to fungus and disease and can rot bulbs. Anything you can do to foster swift drainage is worth doing, such as double digging or adding shredded pine bark, compost, or peat moss.

Double digging is a systematic method of loosening up the soil in the entire bed. Dig a trench about one foot wide and the length of the bed. Set aside the soil. Dig a second trench alongside the first, then shovel the soil from that trench into the first. Repeat across the bed, replacing the soil from the last trench with the soil set aside from the first.

❦ Plant bulbs deep if you'd like them to naturalize. When in doubt, plant deeper. That means digging deep to allow for drainage or creating raised beds. Remember, the bigger the bulb, the deeper the hole.

❦ Water bulbs right after planting. Although they don't like wet feet, they need water to trigger growth.

❦ Bulbs are their own complete storage system and contain all the nutrients they need for one year. When you feed them in the fall, you're promoting next year's growth. Use organic material, compost, or a balanced timed-release bulb food.

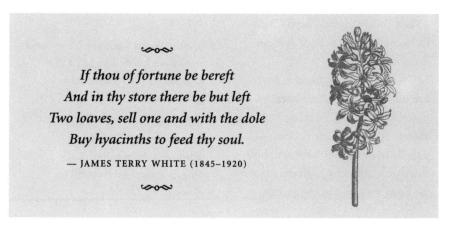

If thou of fortune be bereft
And in thy store there be but left
Two loaves, sell one and with the dole
Buy hyacinths to feed thy soul.

— JAMES TERRY WHITE (1845–1920)

Heirloom Bulbs:
Underground Treasures

*Y*ou might call Scott Kunst of Old House Gardens in Ann Arbor, Michigan, a bulb detective, for his passion is seeking out old bulbs, finding clues to their histories, and solving their mysteries. Some years ago, Kunst noticed that one of his favorite tulips, 'Prince of Austria', a hardy red rebloomer that's also fragrant, had disappeared from the catalogs. He still had it growing, however, and he decided that if he didn't offer it for sale, no one else would. That was the beginning. Now Kunst's mail-order catalog has been called a primer on the history of flower bulbs, and his bulbs are blooming at Old Sturbridge Village in Massachusetts, Monticello in Virginia, Greenfield Village in Michigan, Joslyn Castle in Nebraska, and private gardens everywhere.

Heirloom, or antique, bulbs are survivors. They have been planted and saved for many years — at least 50 or 60 in most cases — usually because they have some distinctive qualities or just because they perform very well in the garden.

OUR PICKS FOR HEIRLOOM BULBS

❧ The 'Sir Watkin' daffodil is very vigorous, long lasting, and cheerful. It was around by 1884 and was once called the "Welsh Giant."

❧ The 'Franciscus Drake' daffodil (1921) is a beautiful gold-and-white flower.

❧ The Tenby daffodil (1631 or 1796) is a small, early-blooming bright yellow trumpet, which has been called the "most perfect in proportion."

❧ For crocuses, try 'Cloth of Gold' (1587), 'Queen of the Blues' (1916), and 'King of the Striped' (1880).

❧ True blue Roman hyacinths, known by 1613, are great for forcing.

❧ Snake's-head fritillary (*Fritillaria meleagris*), listed in 1572, is a checkered lily likened to a guinea hen.

❧ Jacob's ladder (*Polemonium caeroleum*), the hardy gladiolus once called turkey flag, is a perennial north to Zone 6.

Naturalizing Bulbs

A naturalized planting should give the feeling that the plants grew and colonized without a helping hand. For a natural look, plant bulbs of the same variety in irregular groups in a gently sloping area with good drainage — along the banks of a brook or pond, along a path, at the base of a wall or hedge, or under trees and shrubs. Some gardeners like to scatter bulbs in a random fashion and plant them where they fall; if you do, take care not to lose any. Lift the soil with a small spade or use a special hand-held bulb planter to remove a plug of soil. Work carefully around the roots of established trees and shrubs.

Bulbs that are excellent naturalizers include crocuses, colchicums, squills, grape hyacinths, lilies, alliums, glory-of-the-snow, winter aconite, daffodils, snowdrops, and hyacinths.

Fooling Mother Nature: Forcing Bulbs

No matter how deep the snow, gardeners can stage spring with parlor pots of sweet-scented paper whites, old-fashioned hyacinths, and dramatic amaryllis. Start now and don't stop until every windowsill and side table is abloom with potted beauties. It's a sure cure for the wintertime blues.

Forcing is speeding up the growth of a plant or bulb to make it bloom on your own schedule. Forced bulbs can add color and perfume to your home or office from fall to spring. Since bulbs contain all the nutrients they need to grow and bloom, it's not hard to force them. It's a matter of timing and temperature, mimicking winter's dark and cold to encourage root growth and trigger the chemical reaction that leads to flowering, then moving the bulb into strong light, as if spring has come.

Most of us cut our bulb-forcing teeth on amaryllis and paper whites, the easiest bulbs to force. Neither needs cold treatment; they're ready to grow as soon as you buy them. To have bloom in time for Christmas, start about five or six weeks in advance. (See "A Step-by-Step Guide to Forcing Paper Whites" on page 99.)

Most spring bulbs need a period of chilling to simulate winter. Keep them above freezing and below 50° F; 40° to 50° F is perfect. Florists use a temperature-controlled cooler vault; home gardeners can use a root cellar, unheated garage or basement, cold frame, or even a trench dug in the garden, then filled with loose soil and mulched. Some city gardeners find just the right temperature under their front steps. As a last resort, you can always use your refrigerator.

Set bulbs close together in a container with drainage holes and water well. Put a piece of tape with the date written on it on each pot. Most bulbs need at least 12 weeks of moist cold. If you cover pots with a plastic bag, they'll need less watering. After 12 weeks, when bulbs are well rooted, move the pots to a warmer area with low light for a week or two, then move them into a bright, sunny spot and watch them stretch out and bloom — just like magic.

Most spring-blooming bulbs, including hyacinths, daffodils, crocuses, tulips, grape hyacinths, and dwarf irises can be forced using this method. Choose varieties that will force well (usually those that bloom early outside). We recommend 'Christmas Marvel' or 'Red Riding Hood' tulips; tiny 'Tête-à-Tête' or taller 'February Gold' daffodils; *Crocus vernus* 'Joan of Arc', 'Pickwick', or 'Purpureus Grandiflorus'; *Iris reticulata;* or *Muscari latifolium.*

TIPS FOR FORCING BULBS

❦ To get the most impact from a pot of bulbs, plant daffodils or other bulbs in layers. Set the bottom layer snugly into compost or potting soil and cover with soil so that their noses are still showing. Arrange the second layer of bulbs so that they sit between the tips of the lower bulbs. Then add more soil to cover the bulbs completely and firm it with your fingers. Be sure to leave space at the top of the pot for watering and for a layer of coarse sand to help prevent the soil from drying out.

❦ For a weeks-long parade of beautiful bloom, start bulbs at ten-day intervals. Pot a few extra bulbs for holiday gifts.

❦ You can get potted bulbs to bloom again next spring if you keep them well watered and fertilized after they bloom, giving them lots of light until their foliage yellows. Then cut back on watering. When the foliage has withered completely, store the pots in a warm, dry place for the summer and plant the bulbs in the garden in the fall.

❦ If you chill your bulbs in the refrigerator or a root cellar, be sure to keep them away from apples and pears. Ripening fruit releases ethylene gas, which can stunt flowering and growth.

❦ The key to success in forcing bulbs is to keep them in a cool spot out of direct sun, even when they're in bloom (they'll last longer). Too much warmth, especially at first, will result in long, limp leaves and shriveled buds.

A Step-by-Step Guide to Forcing Paper Whites

*P*aper whites *(Narcissus tazetta)* are native to the Mediterranean region, and they hate cold. Never store them in the refrigerator, and give them a warm growing spot near a radiator or stove — they need bottom heat for the best, fastest growth. "Not all paper whites are created equal," says Brent Heath of the Daffodil Mart in Gloucester, Virginia. He recommends 'Jerusalem', 'Israel', and 'Nazareth' for strong stems, big florets, and wonderful fragrance.

1. Set at least five fat, solid narcissus bulbs close together in a shallow pot or a deeper bowl without drainage holes. Fill the container about two-thirds full with fairly coarse potting soil. "It's much better than pebbles and water," Heath says. "They need air to grow, and in soil they can take up moisture without suffocating." For a bright holiday touch, plant narcissus bulbs in a vase full of cranberries.

2. Arrange the bulbs with their points up and fill in around them, leaving the top half exposed. Water well and set in a cool, dark place. Within days, roots will appear, so vigorous that they may shift the soil a little. When you see green shoots, move the container to a cool, very sunny spot.

3. Good light is the secret of upright, strong-stemmed paper whites. You may need to supplement natural light with grow lights or fluorescent lights hung fairly close (within a foot or two).

4. Paper whites grow fast, and in about three weeks you'll have masses of white or yellow cuplike flowers at the ends of slender green stalks. If they threaten to flop over, tie them with a raffia or ribbon bow, or stake them with berried branches from the garden.

It's not easy to recycle narcissuses grown indoors, but it can be done. Allow the foliage to die back naturally and let the soil dry out. Then plant outside. Feed and water to fatten the bulb.

Most bulbs do well in an all-purpose potting soil that's on the sandy side. Here's a recipe for making your own.

2 parts loam   1 part sand or vermiculite
1 part humus

Our Favorite Bulbs &
Our Advice for Growing Them

Allium *Allium* spp.

The great variety in color and form provided by ornamental onions has led to their popularity as garden flowers. Mostly tall (*A. giganteum* grows taller than six feet; the drumstick allium [*A. sphaerocephalum]* to five feet), with global or star-like flowers on the ends of long stems, they bloom in rosy purple, true blue, yellow, mauve, lilac, and white. They keep their blossoms for up to a month. Smaller alliums, which grow to only five or six inches tall, are good for rock gardens.

❦ Plant allium bulbs in spring or fall.

❦ Plant them roots down, tip up, about three inches deep in fertile soil that receives at least half a day of sun.

❦ For best bloom, fertilize the first shoots about ten days after they appear.

❦ Let the leaves wither and die before cutting them back.

Amaryllis *Hippeastrum* spp.

Amaryllis, which is extremely poisonous, is native to the tropical regions of Central and South America. Its name comes from the Greek word meaning "to shine" and was also the name of a shepherdess in Virgil's poetry. Dramatic hybrid amaryllis shoot up to 18 to 20 inches tall (and sometimes even taller), opening three or four large trumpet-shaped blossoms at the end of each hollow stalk. The blossoms (up to ten inches across) are spectacular in shades of red, white, pink, salmon, and orange, as well as stripes and combinations of colors.

For Winter Bloom Indoors

❦ Choose a large, firm bulb with a good number of root initials (swellings) at the base. The largest bulbs produce the most stems and flowers.

❦ Look for striped 'Peppermint', red 'Claret' or 'Winter Joy', or 'Giant White'.

❦ Plant bulbs in mid- to late autumn for winter bloom. The uncommonly beautiful amaryllis has bulbs so big that they're usually grown one to a pot. Use a pot just a bit bigger than the bulb with a drainage hole in the bottom.

❦ For a dramatic effect, set three bulbs, spaced so that they don't quite touch, in a large pot.

❦ For best bloom, water potted bulbs sparingly until the first sprouts appear (about two weeks after you plant the bulb). From then on, the plant needs even moisture to keep its hollow stalk from collapsing.

❦ Keep the plant at about 70° F, and in another four to six weeks, you'll be dazzled by plate-size flowers.

❦ For longer-lasting bloom, remove the flower's anthers (the pollen-bearing tip of the stamen) as soon as it opens.

After the Bloom

❦ As the flowers fade, remove them carefully, leaving the foliage.

❦ After all danger of frost, move the bulb to the garden, setting it two inches deep in rich, loamy soil.

❦ Feed it regularly; a covering of compost or manure will help, as amaryllis are great feeders. Keep feeding until the leaves start to die back; then slowly reduce watering and stop feeding.

❦ In the fall, dig out the bulbs; cure them for a week or so in a cool, dry place; and then repot them to start the cycle all over again.

Canna *Canna* spp.

Of all the flowers our grandmothers grew, cannas, sometimes called Indian shot, may have fallen the farthest from favor. But foliage plants, and bulbs in general, are more popular now than ever before, so perhaps the dramatic canna is due for a revival.

Cannas are among the most colorful summer bulbs — as flamboyant as their tropical American ancestry — and they come in a vast array of flower color, which ranges from bright to pale, and leaf shape and color. The immense, often veined leaves have sheathing leafstalks and come in various shades of green and bronze.

Dwarf cannas (about 18 to 24 inches tall) are easier to fit into smaller gardens, but gardeners still love spectacular, drought-tolerant varieties, which reach a height of more than six feet and give six months of garden drama. Cannas are the mainstays of massed municipal plantings. The aquatic types make superb tall clumps, flower luxuriously, and star in water gardens and wet places.

Turn-of-the-century gardeners so loved cannas that they grew them from seed. Doing so, Ida Bennett counseled in *The Flower Garden* (1903), "the cost is reduced to a mere bagatelle." Growing cannas from seed isn't easy. The germination rate is low, and the seeds have to be filed or given an acid bath to break down their hard coat. It's better to leave propagation to the experts and buy the tubers.

Exotic, tropical creatures, cannas need a lot of sunshine and plenty of water. North of Zone 7, cannas have to be lifted each fall and stored in a cool, moist, frost-free place. If you don't have a cool basement, dig them a special root cellar (about three feet deep) and cover it with burlap or an old rug. Don't let them dry out; if necessary, sprinkle the sand or soil around them with water. In spring, cut the tubers apart with a sharp knife so that each piece contains one eye on a substantial piece of rootstock.

🌿 Cannas can be started in the house in small pots, then moved to the garden, or set directly in rich soil — two to three inches deep, eyes up.

🌿 In the lower South, let cannas grow without moving them until the clumps become very matted. Every three or four years, dig up the clumps in winter, separate the roots, and replant them in well-enriched soil.

Crocus *Crocus* spp.

Famous harbingers of spring, crocuses bloom right out of the snow. They naturalize freely to carpet our yards with cheerful color: white, blue, orange, lavender, purple, yellow, and gold. They're native to the Mediterranean region, from Spain to Afghanistan, and have been grown in Europe since the early 17th century. Victorians loved entire carpet beds of them and forced them inside in pots or ceramic porcupine figures.

🌿 Crocuses like well-drained, sandy soil and moisture during their season of growth and flowering. If their simple needs are met, they come back stronger every year.

❧ Try planting them in the shade of deciduous trees or
shrubs. Their foliage ripens so early that late-spring shade
doesn't disturb them a bit.

❧ They look wonderful planted in swirling ribbons through
the middle of your garden. Set some in a warm spot by a
southern doorstep; they'll bloom before you expect it,
announcing spring.

❧ Plant autumn crocuses, or colchicums, outdoors from
June to August. Plant them three to four inches deep and
eight to nine inches apart where they will get at least half
a day of full sun. Water thoroughly.

Freesia *Freesia* spp.
In all but the warmest zones, this South African native is
chiefly grown indoors. Freesias are a welcome winter bloom
with a strong, sweet fragrance and lovely pastel (white,
yellow, pink, or violet) blossoms.

❧ A chilly atmosphere is especially important when you're
forcing freesias.

❧ In late summer, plant them about one inch deep (about
six bulbs to a five-inch pot), water well, and place in a
cool, sunny place, such as a cold frame or sun porch.
Water lightly until growth appears. After you see
sprouts, water only when the soil feels dry.

❧ Maintain them at about 45° to 50° F indoors, giving them
plenty of sun while they open up (in about 3½ months).

❧ To prevent flopping, you may need to support them with
slender 12-inch stakes or a wire ring.

❧ After flowering, reduce watering and let the foliage die
back. Remove the corms, shaking off excess dirt, and
store in a dark, cool, slightly moist place.

Gladiolus *Gladiolus* spp.
Nothing is more dramatic in summer bouquets than tall,
stately spikes of gladiolus. Today's hybrids have distinctive,
sword-shaped leaves surrounding spikes of luscious flowers
in every color of the rainbow. Gladioli are native to South
Africa and the Mediterranean. The development of modern
hybrids began in the early 19th century, and today there are
hundreds of cultivars.

Gladioli are easy to grow; in fact, they're almost fool-proof. Gladiolus rootstocks are corms, which have a protective fibrous tunic and a prominent basal plate. Corms are not permanent, but are replaced every year by one or more new corms that grow on top of the old. Save the new corms for replanting next year.

❧ Plant corms 6 inches deep and 6 to 12 inches apart in rich, well-drained soil and full sun.

❧ In a garden setting, gladioli look best planted in bold clumps of one color.

❧ For bouquets, plant them in a cutting garden in rows so that the corms almost touch.

❧ They may need to be staked for support against wind. If wind is a problem in your garden, plant them deeper than six inches.

❧ If you stagger planting, putting in corms every two weeks, you can have bloom until fall. Early-spring plantings will bloom in about four months, later plantings in about three months.

❧ Don't let gladioli dry out during their growing season. Feeding them as soon as they poke out of the ground will encourage luscious blooms.

❧ After flowering, let the plants dry out a bit. Tall hybrids are not hardy and must be lifted and stored indoors. Detach the old corm from the new. Clean the new one and store it in a dry, well-ventilated area at about 50° F. Any corms the size of a quarter are worth saving for next season.

❧ In frost-free areas, perennial, winter-hardy varieties make wonderful garden plants.

Glory-of-the-snow *Chionodoxa* spp.

Chionodoxa is a relative newcomer to our gardens. Plant explorers discovered it in 1842 growing in a high mountain meadow in Turkey. It was introduced for cultivation some 30 years later. Well named glory-of-the-snow, it has beautiful star-shaped flowers in blue or white that open in very early spring. It is spectacular in mass plantings and a nice addition to a rock garden.

❧ Plant chionodoxa in early fall, two to three inches deep in well-drained soil.

❦ It prefers full sun but will abide partial shade.

❦ Chionodoxa self-sows and may need occasional dividing.

❦ Typically, chionodoxa blooms with more gusto as the years go by. Don't be disappointed in the first year's bloom, and don't disturb the bulbs.

Grape Hyacinth *Muscari* spp.

Small, perky *M. armeniacum* provides one of the garden's very best blues, as well as a sweet, musky fragrance. Grape hyacinths are not related to true hyacinths. They resemble a tiny bunch of grapes held on six-inch spikes.

❦ Grape hyacinths make excellent companion plants for daffodils and early tulips.

❦ Set out masses of bulbs in the fall. Plant them three inches deep and three inches apart.

❦ Grape hyacinths naturalize readily and are very easy to grow. To naturalize, don't cut the foliage after bloom.

Hyacinth *Hyacinthus* spp.

Fragrant hyacinths are among the best-loved spring bulbs. They have dense, rather formal looking flower spikes in shades of white, pink, blue, yellow, and red on stout stems between firm, almost stiff leaves. All hyacinths are easy to force indoors and are marvelously fragrant.

According to legend, Apollo accidentally killed his young friend Hyacinthus while they were playing quoits (a game like horseshoes). Actually, it was Zephyr's fault: the wind god caused a metal ring to hit Hyacinthus in the head. Apollo was brokenhearted and created the flower from blood spilled on the ground. In the Victorian language of flowers, hyacinth means sport or play, and the blue hyacinth is a symbol of sincerity.

Planting Outdoors

❦ In areas where there's a hard frost, plant bulbs six inches deep and six to eight inches apart in early October. In warmer areas, wait until early or mid-November.

❦ Plant hyacinths in full sun or partial shade.

❦ Good drainage is a must, for the bulbs rot easily if they stand in water.

❦ Mulch in the fall to protect tender spring foliage from frosts.

❦ After the bloom is over, cut off the flower stems and let the foliage dry out.

❦ In the North, hyacinths suffer from alternate freezing and thawing, and flowers get smaller in successive years. Mulch the plants to protect them from hard winters, and be prepared to replace them every two or three years.

Forcing Indoors

❦ Hyacinths are often forced in water alone — you may have seen them in old-fashioned hourglass-shaped vases (available from many catalogs and florists), which show their fine white roots dangling in water. Whether they are grown in water, pebbles, or soil, hyacinths need constant moisture.

❦ Hyacinths need a period of cold temperatures to kick off the biochemical reaction that starts the flowering process. Start them in coolness and dim light, then move them into warmth and bright light.

❦ Buying precooled hyacinths cuts about two weeks off their growing time, making it possible to have Christmas bloom if you start in October.

❦ Dainty Roman hyacinths *(H. orientalis albulus)*, the simpler form with only three or four loosely spaced blue or white spikes, are even easier to force into bloom and are especially pretty.

❦ A hyacinth water-forced indoors will persist outdoors if you plant it early in well-drained soil and fertilize it.

Lily *Lilium* spp.

Lilies star in the summer garden. Some of them blaze with color, others shine in purest white. Most are fragrant. There are more than 100 species of lilies and thousands of named varieties; modern hybridization has made them hardier and more adaptable.

Lilies are loved the world over and have always been associated with magic and mystery. Greek and Roman mythologies mention the lily, as do legends from China and Japan. It has been used as a symbol of peace, as well as of the

Virgin Mary; the Minoan goddess Britomartis; Venus, the Roman goddess of love; and Juno, the queen of the Greek gods. The Madonna lily was planted in the cloister gardens of medieval monasteries, along castle walkways, and in every self-respecting 19th-century cottage garden.

Lilies grow from one to seven feet tall and come in colors from orange and red to pink, yellow, and white. Spectacular star-shaped Asiatic lilies are hardy and especially easy to grow. Fragrant alabaster Madonna lilies and exquisitely shaped calla lilies are dramatic garden features.

- ❦ Buy fresh bulbs with roots and scales that are firm and intact.
- ❦ Since lilies are never completely dormant, it's important to plant them as soon as you get them, in either spring or fall.
- ❦ They like loose, well-drained soil, acid to neutral in composition; plenty of moisture year-round; cool temperatures for their roots; and bright sun for their leaves. A good way to guarantee cool roots is to overplant lilies with annuals or perennials.
- ❦ Lily bulbs produce two sets of roots, one at the base of the bulb and the other at the top, where the plant's stem emerges. In general, they should be planted deeper than most other bulbs, at a depth about three times the vertical diameter of the bulb. The shallow-rooted Madonna lily should be planted only an inch or two deep in late summer. If you have a problem with mice, moles, or groundhogs, you may have to plant lilies in wire baskets.
- ❦ Don' t let water stand on lilies. If the bulbs get waterlogged, they will rot.
- ❦ Lilies that grow more than three feet tall may need to be staked.
- ❦ Don't disturb hardy garden lilies until the clumps are so large that they begin to decline in vigor. Then divide the clumps.
- ❦ Mulch heavily in the fall to protect against thawing and freezing.
- ❦ Lilies can be forced indoors. Use a large pot and plant three or four bulbs deep enough so that roots can form,

leaving room to add soil as the plants grow. After they bloom, gradually dry out the bulbs, clean them, and store them in moist packing material.

I think lilies are more beautiful than orchids. They're very fragrant, and they don't require much care. Also, they look lovely in arrangements.

They take a bed of their own, where I grow tulips and jonquils in the spring. It's at its peak in July. I fertilize them with bone meal when I plant them, in the spring, and again in the summer. I have both tiger lilies and rubrums. I grow a lot of yellow and white lilies, but this year I have one called 'Mona Lisa' that's simply breathtaking. It's pink with deeper pink inside and very fragrant. The heavenly fragrance is ever present.

— Elsie von Maur, Davenport, Iowa

Narcissus (Daffodil) *Narcissus* spp.

Most gardeners can't imagine spring without daffodils, those trumpet-shaped narcissuses with center cups that are as long as or longer than the petals. Jonquils *(N. jonquilla)* have clusters of flowers with shallow cups that contrast with the petals. Heavily scented paper whites *(N. tazetta)* are beloved for their decorative contribution to fall and winter rooms. (For more on forcing paper whites, see page 99.)

In Greek mythology, Narcissus was a vain youth loved by a mountain nymph named Echo. Ignoring her, he spent all his time looking at his own reflection in a pool of water. When Echo faded away, leaving only her voice, the gods changed Narcissus into a flower, condemned to nod at his own reflection forever.

❦ Plant early-, mid-, and late-season varieties to extend bloom.

❦ Favorite varieties include the yellow trumpets of 'King Alfred' and white 'Mount Hood'. Others range in color from pale yellow, apricot, and pale pink to bicolor white and yellow.

❦ Narcissuses are very hardy and are not attractive to moles or mice.

❦ Choose high-quality, firm bulbs. Avoid soft or spongy ones.

❦ Plant bulbs in early fall in any well-drained soil. Plant them at least twice as deep as their size from top to bottom. Choose a sunny spot.

❦ Daffodils are probably the easiest bulbs to naturalize, and because they bloom in early spring, they can be planted under deciduous trees, where they will get plenty of sun until the trees leaf out.

❦ To get a splendid, sweeping show of bloom, think in terms of planting buckets, not handfuls, of bulbs.

❦ Fertilize in fall. Daffodils like rich, moist soil, but they can't tolerate standing water.

❦ After the bloom, snap off the flower heads. Allow at least six weeks for the foliage to die back naturally. If the foliage is cut too soon, the plant will die.

Snowdrop *Galanthus nivalis*

These tiny white flowers truly herald the coming of spring and aren't at all disturbed by a late snowfall. Their nodding blossoms open as the snow melts in January or February, and they are in full bloom until late March.

Of the 14 species, the most commonly seen are the common snowdrop *(G. nivalis)* and the double *G. nivalis* 'Flore Pleno'. The snowdrop's Latin name, *Galanthus,* comes from the Greek words *gala* (milk) and *anthos* (flower). The common name comes from the German word *Schneetropfen* and refers to a style of drop earring popular in the 16th and 17th centuries.

❦ Plant snowdrops in late summer to early fall.

❦ Plant bulbs in masses, two to three inches deep and two to three inches apart, in moist soil and semishade.

❦ In sandy soil, they will increase and last for many years.

Squill *Scilla* spp.

Hardy, true-blue squill has short spikes of bright blue or white bell-shaped or star-shaped flowers. Some varieties have a delicate, sweet fragrance. With its neat, attractive foliage, squill makes a good border or edging plant and looks wonderful naturalized under trees or shrubs.

The Latin name *Scilla* means "I injure," a reference to the poisonous properties of the plant. In particular, red scilla was once used as a rat poison. During the Elizabethan era, starch made from the bulbs was used for stiffening collars. The fanciful Welsh name for squill is cuckoo's boots.

❦ Squill's small, onion-shaped bulb should be planted three to four inches deep in early fall.

❦ In an open, sunny spot it will multiply rapidly.

❦ Squill does best with some midday shade, moisture during the growing season, and a dry resting period afterward.

Tulip *Tulipa* spp.

Tulips arrived in Europe from Turkey in the mid-16th century and were immediately adored, as they have been ever since. They were usually planted in mixed beds of choice specimens, until the rise of Victorian bedding gardens, where they were massed in island beds. Early in this century, gardeners favored pastel shades in formal beds or woven into perennial borders. Tulips come in a great variety of sizes and colors, all with the same basic flower form: six petals and broad green leaves. Hybrid tulip bulbs are larger than those of species tulips.

❦ Buy the biggest, firmest bulbs you can find.

❦ In autumn, plant tulips four to six inches deep in rich, well-aerated soil amended with leaf mold or organic matter. They like full sun or partial shade.

❦ Unless you live in an area with dry summers, you probably can't count on repeat bloom.

❦ To get the longest vase life for a bunch of tulips, cut the stems diagonally, then wrap the bunch in a cone of newspaper and stand them in water (just up to the paper) for an hour or two. When you're ready with a vase, recut the stems, again on the diagonal. Kept out of direct sunlight, heat, and drafts, tulips will last for at least a week.

> *Tulips like to be baked in summer, so plant them very deep and plenty of them. You cannot achieve drama with a two-foot strip along the driveway.*
>
> — Rob Proctor, *The Indoor Potted Bulb* (1993)
> and *The Outdoor Potted Bulb* (1993)

> *The ground must be extremely loose. At our garden, we treat tulips as annuals because we want to have gorgeous big flowers. So we dig, clean, and recycle the bulbs and put in new ones every year. [Home gardeners don't need to do that, but their tulips will produce smaller blooms the second year.]*
>
> — Patsy Sadler, Pella Historical Society, Pella, Iowa

Winter Aconite *Eranthis* spp.

Buttercup-yellow winter aconite, a Eurasian member of the buttercup family, rivals the snowdrop in early bloom and makes a nice companion. Like the other early bloomers, it is just a few inches high. It has large, broad-petaled, honey-scented flowers that seem to pave the garden with sunshine almost overnight. Flower stalks rise from a ruff of finely divided leaves that form clumps.

❧ Winter aconite needs winter low temperatures of at least 20° F and is hardy to −30° F.

❧ The knobby tubers are brittle and should be handled with care. They can be purchased soon after their spring flowering, while still growing; in this case, they should be planted at once. They also can be obtained in a dried state in autumn; soak them for a few hours or overnight before setting them out.

❧ Plant the bulbs in late spring or very early autumn. Set them three to five inches deep and about three inches apart.

❧ Winter aconite grows well in acid soils but prefers alkaline conditions.

❧ It can be naturalized under trees and shrubs, as it doesn't mind shade. In a cool spring, it may bloom for months.

The Bulb Garden

My favorite flowers are the spring garden beauties. We wait so long for winter to end, and then when they finally bloom, they're so beautiful and perfect.

We built a rock garden behind the house. There's a huge arbor with Japanese wisteria and Silver Lace vine, a fast-growing perennial that blooms all summer. It had been a garage, and we had to dig out four feet of cinders. The garden has an hourglass design, and the pathways are made of creek stones. I have at least 500 bulbs planted there, and every year I keep adding more — irises, dwarf daffodils, grape hyacinths, red and pink tulips, late-blooming scented daffodils.

After I plant bulbs in the fall, I sometimes forget where I've put them, so every spring's a surprise. I get an overview from a second-story window. I sit and look out and decide where I need more color. I really enjoy the bulb garden.

— Joan Hendrick, Rochester, New York

Double daffodil
(*Narcissus* spp.)

Chapter 5

Designs, Schemes & Themes

Strength may wield the ponderous spade,
May turn the clod, and wheel the compost home;
But elegance, chief grace the garden shows,
And most attractive, is the fair result
Of thought, the creature of a polished mind.

— *WILLIAM COWPER (1731–1800)*

Bearded Iris
(*Iris germanica*)

*W*ITH ALL THE FLOWER TYPES, COLORS, HEIGHTS, AND characteristics to think about, as well as their particular needs and preferences, how do you combine them to make a garden that is attractive and manageable? Of course, there are whole books on the subject of garden design, and many seed catalogs are now providing plans for gardens in every combination. It is helpful to follow a plan, but remember that it's your garden, and your tastes and preferences will make it original. Your microclimate will dictate successes and failures to a great extent, but you may find that you can grow a flower that theoretically won't work. Don't be afraid to experiment and express yourself.

In this section, we offer some suggestions, and even some plans, to ponder when you are making decisions about what to grow in your garden and how to arrange the flowers you choose. To attract butterflies and hummingbirds, include plants listed in "A Nectar Garden for Winged Things." For those interested in history, we offer "An Early American Parlor Garden," planted in 1992 in celebration of *The Old Farmer's Almanac*'s 200th birthday. Addressing current concerns for water conservation, "The Water-Thrifty Garden" and xeriscaping techniques offer ways in which we can satisfy our thirst for beauty without running the well dry. "The Three-Season Perennial Garden" includes many easy-to-grow favorites and will give a succession of bloom from May through October. For a truly American garden, look to native perennials, bulbs, and ferns listed in "Wildflowers: Following Nature's Lead."

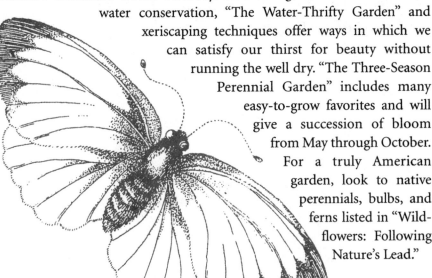

A Nectar Garden for Winged Things

Which came first, the insects or the flowers? While scientists debate this point, gardeners delight in their partnership, which seems to benefit both parties. Nothing is more fascinating than the sight of bees and butterflies — hummingbirds, too — with heads plunged deep inside bright blossoms. Nectar is the reward, and color and fragrance are the lures.

What is nectar? The ancients believed it fell into flowers directly from heaven and named it after the life-giving beverage of the gods. All the bees had to do was collect those heavenly drops and ripen them into honey. Actually, nectar is the sweet, water-based fluid secreted by flowers for its pollinators — neither a waste product nor a sap, but an edible treat made by a gland called the nectary. This gland is positioned where pollinators must probe for it with their tongues. (Honeybees don't suck; they have hairy little spoons at the tip of their long tongues and lap up nectar the way a cat laps milk.) The nectary is protect-ed from rain by hidden hairs or the spurs of flowers such as columbines.

The flowers of different species produce nectars with different sugar concentrations that vary with temperature, climate, the age of the flower, and the water level of the soil. Nectar can be up to 75 percent sucrose, or sugar, but the average sugar content is about 30 to 35 percent. It also contains other compounds and may be acid or alka-line. To supplement their diets, butterflies drink at puddles, for minerals, and love manure tea, which is rich in dissolved salts and sugars.

Flowers need insects, and insects need flowers, but their complex rituals of reciprocity are still being investigated. Commonly held beliefs about the order of evolution — flowers first, then insects — have been contradicted

PLANTS THAT ATTRACT BUTTERFLIES

Allium *(Allium)*
Aster *(Aster)*
Bee balm *(Monarda)*
Butterfly bush *(Buddleia)*
Catmint *(Nepeta)*
Clove pink *(Dianthus)*
Cornflower *(Centaurea)*
Daylily *(Hemerocallis)*
False indigo *(Baptisia)*
Fleabane *(Erigeron)*
Flossflower *(Ageratum)*
Globe thistle *(Echinops)*
Goldenrod *(Solidago)*
Hollyhock *(Alcea)*
Honeysuckle *(Lonicera)*
Lavender *(Lavendula)*
Lilac *(Syringa)*
Lupine *(Lupinus)*
Lychnis *(Lychnis)*

Mallow *(Malva)*
Milkweed *(Asclepias)*
Mint *(Mentha)*
Pansy *(Viola)*
Phlox *(Phlox)*
Privet *(Ligustrum)*
Purple coneflower *(Echinacea)*
Purple loosestrife *(Lythrum)*
Rock cress *(Arabis)*
Sage *(Salvia)*
Sea holly *(Eryngium)*
Shasta daisy *(Chrysanthemum)*
Snapdragon *(Antirrhinum)*
Sneezeweed *(Helenium)*
Stonecrop *(Sedum)*
Sweet alyssum *(Lobularia)*
Sweet rocket *(Hesperis)*
Tickseed *(Coreopsis)*
Zinnia *(Zinnia)*

by the recent work of paleontologists Conrad C. Labandiera and J. John Sepkoski. Their analyses of fossil records show that insects evolved long before flowering plants and just stuck around. Flowers came into a world full of sippers and chewers, borers and crushers — insects already hungry for nearly 100 million years.

But the appearance and spread of flowers took place a good 125 million years ago, and the many species that are not wind-pollinated depend on bees and other insects for the transfer of their pollen and the perpetuation of their kind. Their reciprocal evolution is long-standing, and their mutuality is a familiar sight in the garden today.

What causes a butterfly to prefer one flower over another? The answer must have something to do with butterfly anatomy. Butterflies take up nectar with a tubelike proboscis (like a soda straw except that it can be coiled up when not in use), so they fancy flowers with tubular nectar sources. They also have extremely long legs and need a platform to land on. Many of the best butterfly flowers are not single blossoms but clusters of small blossoms arranged in a horizontal plane, such as yarrow, Queen Anne's lace, and members of the Compositae family (such as daisies). This arrangement saves butterfly energy. A butterfly can load up on the nectar of many individual blossoms from one vantage point without having to flit from blossom to blossom.

Bees, too, are models of efficiency when it comes to nectaring. They start with the lowest flower on a stalk and climb upward in a continuous spiral while poking their tongues into each blossom along the way. Once the bee makes it to the top blossom, it flutters down to the next flower and starts all over again. Since climbing up takes less energy than flying up, it's a calorie-saving approach.

A garden of fragrance, flowers, and fruits provides an inviting habitat for birds as well as butterflies and bees. All these creatures need fresh water, some shelter, sunny open spaces, and lots of flowers. Wildflower gardens provide a natural landscape that insects and birds find irresistible, especially if there is a pond or brook nearby. Creating a variety of habitats is important if you want to entice a diversity of species. Herb gardens attract insects and birds. Include plenty of parsley, dill, and fennel for the black swallowtail caterpillars. (It's important to realize that without certain host plants, butterflies will not lay eggs. They choose plants that will provide food for their larvae. These plants are usually wildflowers.)

[The] flowers set their caps for passing bees, appealing to every instinct and appetite — sensory, dietetic and comfort.
They hung out banners and flags of the favorite colors of the insects, they shamelessly sprayed the air with alluring perfumes, and spread buffet luncheons with nutritious and sweet nectar. The susceptible bee alighted on the colored carpet of welcome, and found a wide, easy way to the banquet.

— WILLIAM BEEBE (1877–1962)

Hummingbirds on the prowl are particularly fond of bright (red, orange, and fuchsia), trumpet-shaped blooms. They love honeysuckle, red-hot poker, bee balm, and cypress vine, with its proliferation of red trumpets. Tiny hummingbirds consume half their weight in nectar every day, so give them lots of flowers. Butterflies are particularly fond of buddleias, commonly called butterfly bush, which bees also relish.

FLOWERS THAT ATTRACT HUMMINGBIRDS

Beardtongue *(Penstemon)*
Bee balm *(Monarda)*
Butterfly bush *(Buddleia)*
Catmint *(Nepeta)*
Clove pink *(Dianthus)*
Columbine *(Aquilegia)*
Coral-bells *(Heuchera)*
Daylily *(Hemerocallis)*
Flowering tobacco
   (Nicotiana alata)
Foxglove *(Digitalis)*
Larkspur *(Consolida)*
Lily *(Lilium)*

Lupine *(Lupinus)*
Petunia *(Petunia)*
Pincushion flower *(Scabiosa)*
Red-hot poker *(Kniphofia)*
Scarlet sage *(Salvia splendens)*
Scarlet trumpet honeysuckle
   (Lonicera × brownii)
Soapwort *(Saponaria)*
Summer phlox
   (Phlox paniculata)
Verbena *(Verbena)*
Weigela *(Weigela)*
Yucca *(Yucca)*

Note: Choose varieties in red and orange shades.

Cultivating Young Flower Gardeners

"Do not think it a waste of time to cultivate a few flowers or to let the children have a flower bed. It is judicious for parents to cultivate a love of flowers in their children from earliest years, as flowers have a refining influence, and never lead astray, but always upward to what is purer and better. If one's time and strength are limited, a bed one yard square, with a geranium and a few nasturtiums, for instance, can give pleasure to the whole household; and these flowers will bloom all the season, until the frost blights them. A few flowers in pots are better than none."

— *The Old Farmer's Almanac,* 1893

Children love sunflowers. The seeds are large and can be poked into the earth one by one to a depth of about an inch. Some children we know have a magical "Sunflower House," a living playhouse of sunflowers planted in a rectangle and interplanted with morning glories guided by a lattice of twine to form a roof.

An Early American Parlor Garden

When the Pilgrims established the first colonial gardens at Plymouth in the spring of 1621, they hastily turned over the ground near their houses and planted the precious seeds and cuttings brought from England. These "cottage," or kitchen, gardens — filled higgledy-piggledy with vegetables and utilitarian herbs — remained the prototype for all but the wealthiest colonists right through the Revolutionary War.

In addition to the plants carried over from England, the gardener of the late 18th century, most likely a woman, would have been familiar with native plants and introduced them into her garden. For bee balm and lupines, for instance, she had only to gather plants from the countryside. During the more than 150 years since those first Pilgrim gardens, New England gardeners had learned to adapt their English traditions to the climate and soil of the New World, and they had adopted many new plants.

After the Revolution, Americans celebrated their hard-won political independence and expressed their freedom in any way possible. For American gardeners this meant creating a unique style, one that would strike a balance between the order and structure of elaborate European gardens on the one hand and the good sense of using native plants (many with medicinal properties) and garden designs suitable for the new United States on the other hand. It was at this time, roughly the 1790s, that the American parlor garden came into vogue.

The parlor garden had several important characteristics.

🌺 It was always fenced, both to maintain privacy and to keep out animals. In urban areas, solid board fences were common; in rural areas, lattice and picket fences were favored.

🌺 The garden usually ran the full width of the house and extended toward the road about two-thirds that distance (because many houses were 36 feet wide, 36x24 feet was a common size for parlor gardens). It generally had a central path that led from the road to the front door of the house; side paths branched off at right or acute angles. There was almost always a gate at the entrance. The paths, surfaced

The Water-Thrifty Garden

There's a new concept in gardening sweeping the land. Well, perhaps it's not new, for thriftiness has been one of the gardener's guiding principles since Adam first lifted a spade. But our need to use less water is a challenge facing gardeners all over the country. The challenge is in response to a real crisis, for we are running out of water — or at least the demand is outstripping the supply. In the last 200 years, cities have grown, population has grown, water use has increased tremendously, and we have been profligate with natural resources. Looking to the future, we must conserve water, and the need to do so has become the driving force in what has been called a backyard revolution and even a gardening renaissance. The crisis is stimulating extraordinary inventiveness. Gardeners are reviving old, forgotten techniques and inventing new ones.

CHOOSE DROUGHT-RESISTANT PLANTS

Native plants and wildflowers are obvious candidates for water-saving gardens. Mainly perennials, they include fuzzy lamb's ears, pink hollyhock mallow, black-eyed Susans, coreopsis, pussytoes and other daisies, feverfew, yarrow, and, later in the summer, milkweed, purple coneflower, statuesque Queen Anne's lace, goldenrod, and fall asters. Some may call these weekend-garden favorites weeds; in this case, a weed is a plant that thrives when others perish.

One of the garden stalwarts, sedum, is so tough that it's commonly called stonecrop. Old-fashioned feverfew flowers rampantly all summer, and yarrow, also called sneezewort, seems to thrive on neglect. (Take another look at the common white yarrow. It's lovely in masses and even pretty when dried.) Consider bold, long-lasting blue globe thistle, which is so self-reliant it often stands guard at deserted farmsteads. Once started, the annuals cleome and portulaca (one tall, the other trailing) are very drought tolerant, as are many herbs, including creeping thyme, tansy, hyssop, wormwood, and chamomile.

Globe thistle
(*Echinops spinosa*)

> ⧼⧽
>
> *These are the gardens of the Desert, these*
> *The unshorn fields, boundless and beautiful,*
> *For which the speech of England has no name —*
> *The Prairies.*
>
> — WILLIAM CULLEN BRYANT (1794–1878)
>
> ⧼⧽

"Think of plants that grow at the seashore or on mountaintops," advises an experienced gardener. "They have the most drought resistance, as they suffer those desiccating winds." Following this lead, we might plant creeping juniper, perhaps the cultivar 'Bar Harbor', for coast-of-Maine hardiness; silvery beach wormwood; or *Rosa rugosa,* sometimes called saltspray rose. Drought-hardy mountain bluet blooms all summer in a friend's Catskill Mountain garden where water is in short supply. I've seen butter-yellow cinquefoil (potentilla) flowering near glaciers on the slopes of New Hampshire's Mount Washington; it's adaptive in a rock garden or as a ground cover in most parts of the country.

Many plants native to desert and Mediterranean-zone soils also adapt widely. Cacti, agaves, and yuccas — desert standards familiar as houseplants — do well in dry gardens from coast to coast. *Yucca filamentosa* is an American native common in eastern gardens from Miami to Maine, where it provides fragrant, night-blooming bell-shaped flowers in summer and structural interest in winter. Deep-rooted yucca ignores dry seasons and may outlive generations of gardeners. In the North, prickly pear cactus withstands frost but needs protection from accumulated snow and ice. Sempervivums, which have dozens of curious names, including Aaron's rod, Jove's-beard, and hen-and-chickens, are undemanding succulent perennials that look like desert creatures. In fact, they thrive in any lean, gritty soil, unfazed by drought and heat.

The fragrant, woody perennial herbs rosemary and lavender, native to Mediterranean zones, thrive in dry gardens in the American West. Other world travelers that thrive in California gardens (or any wet-winter, dry-summer places) include cascading basket-of-gold *(Aurinia saxatilis);* evergreen, daisy-like cotton lavender *(Santolina chamaecyparissus);* and hardy

Madagascar periwinkle *(Catharanthus roseus)*; with its clear flowers and shiny, waxy leaves.

California gardeners planting xeriscapic, low-maintenance gardens have hundreds of native species to consider. Sunny California poppies *(Eschscholzia californica)* and orange butterfly weed, the showiest native milkweed, add jolts of color, as well as attracting all sorts of butterflies. Native meadow flowers such as blue flax, Mexican hats, and mule-ears are ideal for dry, open spots. Most *Ceanothus* species, those wonderful wild lilacs that turn the hills blue in early spring, are native to California. Whether low growing like Carmel creeper or shrubby like San Diego Sierra blue, they are beautifully drought tolerant. Manzanitas, another family of hardy evergreen shrubs, also range from diminutive to massive and make excellent ground covers for dry slopes. One, Little Sur manzanita, is a close relative of the kinnikinnick (bearberry), hardy north to Zone 3, which was smoked like tobacco by Indians and pioneers in the Great Lakes region. This connection seems curious, unless you think of them both as survivors — the fittest of plants, versatile, and admirably stress adapted.

XERISCAPING

Xeriscaping, or choosing plants that thrive in or can adapt to a dry environment, is a trend that is attracting many followers. Here are some tips for xeriscaping in your garden.

- Choose drought-resistant plants, especially natives.
- Group plants with similar water requirements. Set species with greater water needs in depressions to collect water when it rains.
- Use mulch to conserve moisture.
- Reduce the area of your lawn. Consider instead ornamental grasses or ground covers.
- Take advantage of runoff from roofs and driveways. Reuse wastewater whenever possible.
- Water gardens deeply and infrequently, rather than encouraging shallow roots by frequent watering.
- Improve the soil's water-holding capacity by using a waterholding gel near roots.
- Install specific, highly efficient irrigation systems, such as drip irrigation.

Kinnikinnick
(Arctostaphylos uva-ursi)

The Three-Season Perennial Garden

To help you get a perennial border started, we offer the following tried-and-true design. It's one of our favorites, since it includes a number of easy-to-grow plants and considers a succession of bloom to bring color to your garden from May through October. (You could, of course, tuck in some daffodils and early tulips here and there for color in April as well.) Follow this design plant by plant, or use it to get some ideas for your own combinations. We have not specified varieties; the fun of making choices is all yours.

The garden is laid out as a 27-foot border, half of which promises always to dazzle with its display. You can, of course, adapt some ideas for a smaller border.

For each of the flowering periods, one special type of plant predominates. In late spring, various irises highlight the display. The early-summer garden depends on delphiniums, late summer emphasizes phlox, and fall gets its glory from asters.

THE GARDEN DESIGN

Refer to this planting plan for suggestions on what goes where. Each square on the plan represents one square foot of space. The number of plants for each location is indicated in parentheses following the plant name.

1. Siberian iris, tall white (2)
2. German iris, tall yellow (3)
3. German iris, tall purple (2)
4. Siberian iris, medium-tall blue (1)
5. German iris, medium-tall mauve (3)
6. Siberian iris, tall blue (2)
7. German iris, medium mahogany (2)
8. Phlox, tall lavender (1)
9. Phlox, tall pink (7)

9   11   12   6   19

1   2   8   3   4   5   13   25   17

15   22   20   23

21   14   26   7

27   24   28

10

10. Dianthus, pink (6), intermixed with balloon flower, dwarf blue (6), and catmint (6)
11. Phlox, tall white (3)
12. Phlox, tall red (3)
13. Phlox, medium pink (3)
14. Daylily, early low yellow (1)
15. Daylily, early low pink (1)
16. Lupine, pink (4)
17. Lupine, yellow (5)
18. Phlox, tall white (2)
19. Tiger lily (4)
20. Coral-bells (2)
21. Shasta daisy (3)
22. Phlox, medium salmon (4)
23. Phlox, low pink, dark-eyed (3)
24. Statice (3)
25. 'Silver King' artemisia (1)
26. Salvia, red (1)
27. Veronica, blue (5)
28. Veronica, blue (2)
29. Meadow rue (1)
30. Regal lily (7)
31. Leadwort (4), interplanted with golden flax (6)
32. Leadwort (6), interplanted with golden flax (6)
33. Chrysanthemum, pink (2)
34. Aster, red (1)
35. Aster, pink (1)
36. Aster, white (1)
37. Aster, pink (1)
38. Sea lavender (1)
39. Shasta daisy (1)
40. Sea lavender (8)
41. Lily, orange (1)
42. Lily, orange (2)
43. Lily, orange (8)
44. Hardy aster, medium red (2)
45. Hardy aster, medium pink (2)
46. Hardy aster, tall white (2)
47. Hardy aster, tall blue (1)
48. Hardy aster, tall white (1)
49. Sneezeweed, yellow (1)
50. Hardy aster, tall lavender (2)
51. Delphinium, blue (4)
52. Hardy aster, tall white (1)
53. Hybrid delphinium, blue (4)
54. Hybrid delphinium, purple (4)
55. Hybrid delphinium, deep blue (8)

From "The Three-Season Perennial Garden" by Jessica Barlow, *The Old Farmer's Almanac HomeOwners Companion*, 1997.

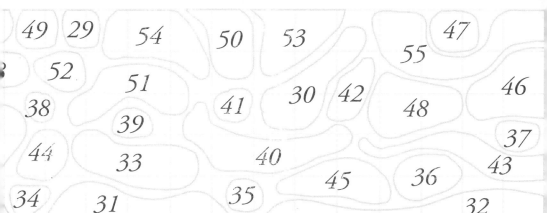

Wildflowers:
Following Nature's Lead

Wildflowers make themselves at home when they're happily married to the soil and climatic conditions in which they've evolved. Suitability is the key to success in growing wildflowers. When the choice of plant is right, they're easy to grow.

We have more than 6,000 native species growing all across America. Some are drought tolerant, and some prefer wet or boggy spots. There are natives for almost every type of soil, as well as those that can withstand searing heat, bitter cold, and gale-force winds. It's up to you to choose wild plants that suit your situation. Don't try to grow sun lovers like black-eyed Susans in a shady spot or shy (but stunning) bloodroot in full sun. Get to know what's native to your area and follow nature's lead.

The idea of meadow gardening probably evolved from midwestern enthusiasm for restoring natural prairies. And in that part of the country, plantings of native grasses and prairie flowers often do very well, even when gardeners reverse the natural equation of 75 percent grasses and 25 percent flowers.

The National Wildlife Research Center in Austin, Texas, stresses the importance of shopping at reputable native-plant nurseries rather

> ∾⊙∽
>
> *To see the world in a grain of sand,*
> *And a heaven in a wild flower;*
> *Hold infinity in the palm of your hand,*
> *And eternity in an hour.*
>
> — WILLIAM BLAKE (1757–1827)
>
> ∾⊙∽

than kidnapping plants from the wild. Collecting wild plants has already seriously diminished and even eliminated whole colonies of natives, and it's not even very successful. Plants dug up from the wild usually don't have enough of their root ball and don't survive transportation shock. But the future is bright. There is a small but growing industry in native-plant nurseries artfully propagating plants from seed. Find one in your area; it's best to use plants propagated from wild populations within 50 miles (or as close as possible) of your garden.

Before you design a wildflower garden or spend any money on plants or seeds, you must understand the character of your site and your soil. (If you don't know whether your soil is acid or alkaline, get it tested.) When shopping, be aware of the phrase *nursery grown*. This may mean dug from the wild and grown for a while in the nursery before being sold. Look for plants that are *nursery propagated* and don't be misled.

Growing wildflowers is a fun way to garden, but it'll work only if you use indigenous seeds or plants and if you're prepared to take care of your garden. Meadow gardening is an ongoing process. Your meadow will look messy at times. You're working with nature, and nature isn't always beautiful. It goes through dormancy.

— Laura Martin, Atlanta, Georgia

PROMISING PLANTS FOR THE 21ST CENTURY

The following recommendations of widely adaptable native plants were made by experts at a symposium held in 1995 at the Brooklyn Botanic Garden.

Native Perennials

Claire Sawyer is director of the Scott Arboretum at Swarthmore College, formerly horticulturist at the Mount Cuba Center. Her list of choice perennials includes her personal favorites for fall. "Fall peak is an American garden strength," she reminds us.

Blue star *(Amsonia hubrectii)*

Cabbage-leaf coneflower *(Rudbeckia maxima)*

Catchfly *(Silene polypetala* and *S. polypetala × virginica)*

Compass plant *(Silphium laciniatum)*

Cup plant *(Silphium perfoliatum)*

Indian pink *(Spigelia marilandica)*

Ladies' tresses orchid *(Spiranthes odorata* and *S. cernua odorata)*

New England aster *(Aster novae-angliae* 'Purple Dome')

Stonecrop *(Sedum ternatum)*

Wild ginger *(Hexastylis [Asarum] shuttleworthii* 'Callaway')

Native Geophytes (Bulbs)

Judy Glattstein is a Connecticut garden designer and author of *The American Gardener's World of Bulbs* (Little, Brown, 1994). Her list of native bulbs may win your heart. Just try them, she says.

Bloodroot *(Sanguinaria canadensis)*

Canada lily *(Lilium canadense)*

Crinum lily *(Crinum americanum)*

Desert lily *(Hesperocallis undulata)*

Dutchman's breeches *(Dicentra cucullaria)*

Jack-in-the-pulpit *(Arisaema triphyllum* 'Mrs. French')

Spider lily *(Hymenocallis liriosome)*

Whippoorwill flower *(Trillium cuneatum)*

Yellow trillium *(Trillium luteum)*

Native Ferns

C. Colston Burrell designs landscapes with native plants in Minneapolis, Minnesota. The greatest obstacle to the wide acceptance of native gardens, he says, is fear of an untidy yard. Conquer that fear with a strong design. Then fill it with exuberant plants and ferns that have long been neglected in home gardens.

Broad beech fern *(Dryopteris [Thelypteris] hexagonoptera)*

Deer fern *(Blechnum spicant)*

Five-finger maidenhair fern *(Adiantum aleuticum)*

Glade fern *(Diplazium [Athyrium] pycnocarpon)*

Goldie's fern *(Dryopteris goldiana)*

Interrupted fern *(Osmunda claytoniana)*

Lady fern *(Athyrium filix-femina* 'Frizelliae' and 'Victoriae')

Maiden fern *(Thelypteris kunthii)*

Male fern *(Dryopteris filix-mas)*

Narrow beech fern *(Phegopteris connectilis)*

Rusty woodsia
  (Woodsia ilvensis)

Male fern
(Dryopteris filix-mas)

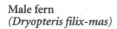

Design Tips from the Experts

DAYLILY COMPANIONS

We combine daylilies with everything from raspberries to rhubarb. We've got them growing with roses, with vegetables, near beanpoles. They ask little and return a lot in terms of color, and they live — as far as we know — forever!

— Lee Bristol, Sherman, Connecticut

BORDER PATROL

Borders for flowers should never be made too narrow. Five or six feet is a good width, while eight feet is better. Beds two to three feet wide suffer in dry weather and give less opportunity for grouping plants. One bed six feet wide is much better than two three feet wide.

— *The Old Farmer's Almanac,* 1914

KEEP 'EM CLOSE

A good idea for impact is to plant flowers somewhat closer together than usual. This forces them to compete and fill in, and they tend to grow a little taller. Impatiens, for instance, should never be planted too far apart.

— Michael Warhurst, Prescott Park, Portsmouth, New Hampshire

FILL IN THE BLANKS

Blank spaces occur in flower borders when bulbs like tulips and narcissuses die down, or after such plants as lungwort and Oriental poppies have lost their foliage. Sow seeds of poppies, calendula, and sweet alyssum in April, when the bulbous plants are just coming up, and have a reserve bed of seedlings like zinnias or marigolds, which can easily be transplanted into the vacant spaces. Bedding plants such as heliotrope, salvia, or rose geranium can also be used for this purpose.

— *The Old Farmer's Almanac,* 1914

A PLACE FOR EVERYTHING

I use perennial carnations as an edging between the flagstone path and the planting rows. Gladioli have a special row to themselves. Instead of staking them with bamboo canes, which is tedious, I support their tall spikes by planting busy 'Lady' marigolds around them. I grow alpine plants in the cracks between the flagstone path to soften its hard lines and provide a contrast between the mostly taller-growing annuals.

I also plant in special color harmonies. For example, orange-flowered 'Lady' marigolds next to a row of violet heliotrope 'Marine'; yellow cosmos next to blue salvia; red poppies between blue larkspur and blue cornflowers; red snapdragons next to pink asters.

— Derek Fell, Bucks County, Pennsylvania

COLOR HARMONY

In the garden, blue flowers should be placed next to orange, violet next to yellow, while red and pink should be surrounded by green or by white. White may also be dispersed among groups of blue and orange and violet and yellow flowers. Plants whose flowers are to produce a contrast should be of the same size.

— *The Old Farmer's Almanac*, 1906

California poppy
(*Eschscholzia californica*)

Flower Carpets

*T*he notion of a carpet of flowers has a firm grasp on the gardener's imagination.

In the mid-19th century, when annuals from all over the world began to be collected, grown, and enjoyed by gardeners in Europe and America, they were frequently started in greenhouses, sometimes in vast quantities, and then transplanted to outdoor beds in elaborate, formal geometric patterns. These brilliant, extravagant plantings came to be known as carpet beds, after the handwoven Oriental carpets that were in vogue at the time. Carpet beds were grown in public parks and gardens, but also in private yards. Just after the Civil War, "bedding out," as it was called, was hailed as the "modern style," and growing flowers was believed to elevate and purify the soul, even in the pages of *The Old Farmer's Almanac.*

The bedding craze depended on many compact, uniform plants that could be planted in straight lines or crisp blocks. Plantings were some-times renewed or replaced several times during the course of a season and required constant clipping and tending, making the process extremely labor-intensive, as well as time-consuming, difficult, and expensive.

On average, 4,000 plants were used to fill a 100-square-foot garden. In 1886, one garden in Long Branch, New Jersey, held 1.5 million plants, reportedly arranged so artistically that they could be mistaken, at a distance, for carpets laid out to dry on the lawn. In fact, so the story goes, an innocent farmer, passing by with his wife during a storm, turned in to warn the servants to take in the carpets before they were ruined.

Today, although you may see examples of such intricate beds in some public parks and gardens, few home gardeners have the time or inclination to create patterned beds. We wonder, though, if the current popularity of wildflower carpets, meadow gardens, and flowering ground covers may not be seen as an expression of the carpet bed tradition.

Chapter 6

Harvesting Flowers

The pleasure of picking a few flowers and finding the right vase for them is incomparable.

— MAY SARTON (1912–1995)

*F*LOWERS ARE FLEETING, AND EVERY FLOWER LOVER WHO contemplates bloom will soon connive to extend it. Whether by cutting flowers to carry them closer to the hearth or the center of the table, drying them for long-lasting arrangements, or putting them to practical use — to add color to foods or fabrics, to perfume rooms or repel insects — we harvest blooms to reap a second reward.

Some gardeners act like flower farmers, planning and planting crops of flowers specifically for harvest. Others glean blooms from the bounty of midsimmer and fall. Either way, harvesting flowers is a delightful endeavor from start to finish, satisfying our thrifty souls as it tickles our sensibilities.

The Cutting Garden

If you crave armloads of flowers, love to share your best blooms with friends and neighbors, or suffer garden guilt when you raid your display beds, you're ready for a cutting garden.

What is a cutting garden? It's a garden grown just to supply beautiful flowers for bouquets. Unlike a display garden, which has to be maintained faithfully to make a show for as many months as possible, a cutting garden is a flower factory, designed for production and harvest. Whether you start with seedlings, seeds, or bulbs, the idea is to raise the biggest, prettiest blossoms and then pick them — at their peak — to enjoy from a new perspective.

Growing flowers just for harvest is an old-fashioned idea that has gained new popularity. On grand Victorian estates, gardeners tended special gardens to supply flowers for salvers and sideboards, but flower lovers everywhere have always set aside a bit of space to grow favorite flowers for bouquets.

PUTTING IN A CUTTING GARDEN

Properly planned, a cutting garden can yield a supply of bouquets for all seasons — even winter, if you include a bush with bright berries or a gorgeous Chinese redbud. You can grow bulbs for early spring and a variety of perennials that will bloom in succession all summer and fall. Many annuals bloom continuously from late spring to early fall, as long as you keep them picked — and that's the fun part, after all.

A cutting garden needn't be large. Even a bed as small as five by ten feet planted with bright annuals and a few long-blooming perennials can yield a surprising number of bouquets. If you have room for a larger bed, be sure that you have access to all of it, so that you can reach every plant to tend and pick it.

Choose a spot for a cutting garden that gets at least six hours of unobstructed sunlight a day. (If you don't have much sun, choose shade-tolerant plants such as lady's-mantle, columbines, bee balm, or wishbone flower.) Have a source of water nearby: flowers require lots to drink. Plant the flowers in rows or blocks to make the best use of space, and mulch around the bed to discourage weeds and keep your feet dry.

Now think like a farmer. To grow a bumper crop of blossoms, you want the best, most fertile soil possible. Loosen the soil to a depth of at least eight inches. Add compost, manure, or another fertilizer, mixing it in well. If your soil is unbalanced (too acid or too alkaline), add minerals to improve it. (A soil test is always a wise investment; any soil can be improved, once you understand what it needs.)

Choosing what to grow is a delightful process. Consider the colors and the particular flowers you love, the rooms you want to fill, and, of course, what grows best in your climate. Include a variety of flower forms — some spiky, some global, some open and branching — and a mixture of sizes and textures. Good foliage is a plus, but it's easy to find in the yard or garden. You may want to include flowers such as carnations, stock,

GOOD CUTTING ANNUALS

Baby's breath *(Gypsophila elegans)*. A good filler, fresh or dried. Sow several times for continuous bloom.

Bachelor's button *(Centaurea cyanus)*. Also perennial types. Fertilize well.

Blue lace flower *(Trachymene coerulea)*. Graceful, lacy umbels.

China aster *(Callistephus chinensis)*. Each plant is a whole bouquet.

Chinese forget-me-not *(Cynoglossum amabile)*. Starry blossoms; gray-green foliage.

Cosmos *(Cosmos spp.)*. Lacy foliage; many colors.

Dahlia *(Dahlia* spp.)*. Grows from tuber. Great variety in color and form.

Globe amaranth *(Gomphrena globosa)*. Hardy. Pinch back for fullness.

Lantana *(Lantana* spp.)*. Shrubby perennial in some zones. It has rings of florets that change color.

Larkspur *(Consolida ambigua)*. Will self-sow; cut when one-third open.

Lavatera *(Lavatera* spp.)*. Lustrous, chalice-shaped blossoms in blue or rose.

Mexican sunflower *(Tithonia rotundifolia)*. Tall; fast growing.

Nicotiana *(Nicotiana* spp.)*. Red, pink, purple, green, or white.

Phlox *(Phlox drummondii)*. Many colors; fast growing.

Salvia *(Salvia farinacea)*. Long spikes of blue or white; good dried.

Snapdragon *(Antirrhinum* spp.)*. Perennial in some zones. Brilliant, vigorous blossoms.

Stock *(Matthiola* spp.)*. Long spikes of single or double flowers; many colors.

Sweet pea *(Lathyrus odorata)*. A vine; train on stakes or a trellis.

Zinnia *(Zinnia* spp.)*. Great variety in color and form.

or nicotiana just for their ability to add fragrance to a bouquet. Or you may want to grow "everlastings," such as strawflowers, Chinese lantern plant (winter cherry), or statice, which can be air-dried for year-round arrangements.

> ∾
>
> *I'd rather have roses on my table than diamonds on my neck.*
>
> — EMMA GOLDMAN (1869–1940)
>
> ∾

Annuals (flowers that reach maturity from seed in one season) are ideal for cutting gardens because they bloom profusely and keep on producing new flowers when you cut the open ones. If you think of annuals as racehorses, determined to reach the finish line — producing seed — you'll understand why they're repeat bloomers. It's a good idea to raise a second-string crop of annuals in flats, ready to transplant into the cutting garden when flowering starts to slacken on the first crop. If you're growing annuals from seed, use good, fresh seeds and start them inside, according to package directions, for earlier bloom.

Most nurseries and garden centers sell seedlings of popular annuals, complete with basic instructions for their culture. If you use transplants, look for healthy plants with no signs of being root-bound, water them immediately after settling them into the garden, and give them protection from wind and strong sun for the first few days. Self-sowing annuals such as poppies, larkspurs, and nicotiana are always welcome in the cutting garden. Tulips and other spring bulbs make great bouquets; treat tulips like annuals and toss the bulbs after you've harvested the flowers.

The advantage to perennials is that they don't have to be set out every year, but in general they require more room and have a shorter blooming period than annuals. Choose long-blooming perennials such as Shasta daisies, feverfew, and loosestrife, which produce flowers for the better part of the summer. Dahlias, which are tender perennials in cooler zones, are well worth growing for their vast array of colors and forms. And don't forget roses, which make beautiful bouquets. Plant a row in full sun and dedicate it to cutting.

Whatever flowers you decide to raise, you'll reap your reward every time you go out to the cutting garden and harvest dozens of fresh flowers that you grew yourself.

GOOD CUTTING PERENNIALS

Black-eyed Susan *(Rudbeckia fulgida)*. Range of colors; abundant blooms.

Blanket flower *(Gaillardia × grandiflora)*. Also annuals. Bicolored daisies.

Bleeding heart *(Dicentra spectabilis)*. Pink or white; pretty foliage; self-sows.

Coral-bells *(Heuchera sanguinea)*. Delicate bells on slender stalks.

Delphinium *(Delphinium* hybrids)*. Glorious blues, pinks, and whites.

Gooseneck loosestrife *(Lysimachia clethroides)*. Vigorous, graceful cones of small white flowers.

Iris *(Iris* spp.)*. Grows from bulb or rhizome. Vast variety.

Lily *(Lilium* spp.)*. Grows from bulb. Annual in some zones. Both Asiatic and Oriental.

Painted lady *(Chrysanthemum coccineum* or *Tanacetum coccineum)*. Long stems; many colors.

Peony *(Paeonia* spp.)*. Giant blooms; hundreds of varieties.

Purple coneflower *(Echinacea purpurea)*. Long lasting; hardy.

Rose *(Rosa* spp.)*. Wonderful variety.

Salvia *(Salvia azurea grandiflora)*. Deep blue spires.

Shasta daisy *(Chrysanthemum × superbum)*. Long blooming; tall stalks.

Sweet William *(Dianthus barbatus)*. Also annuals. Many colors; spicy scent.

Yarrow *(Achillea* spp.)*. New pastels, as well as gold and white.

YOUR CUTTING GARDEN

❦ Most flowers love sun, so plant your cutting garden in a spot that gets at least six hours of full sun every day.

❦ Don't rush annual seedlings out to the garden. Most annuals love hot weather and don't grow much until the soil is warm. Plants set out in late June or early July will soon catch up with those set out earlier.

❦ Cooperate with Mother Nature. Some plants tolerate dryness; others need damp soil. Some like acid or alkaline soil, full sun or semishade. Research the specific needs of your favorite flowers.

❦ The nearer your garden is to your back door, the easier it will be to maintain.

❦ If you already have a vegetable garden, consider devoting a few beds or rows to growing flowers.

❦ Look around your existing gardens for flowers and foliage to add to bouquets. Don't overlook ivies, ferns, hostas, leafy or flowering shrubs, climbing roses, herbs (mint, lavender, or sage), trailing vines, ornamental grasses, and ground covers (lily of the valley or violets).

❦ Bulbs make great cut flowers. You may decide to devote your cutting garden to summer annuals that follow a crop of spring tulips, daffodils, fritillaries, lilies, and other beauties. When you've cut the bulbs' flowers, pull them and toss them, then prepare the soil for annuals.

❦ Pick frequently.

MAKING FLOWERS LAST

❦ Don't let the stems dry out. Carry a bucket of water right to the garden. Cut stems at an angle with a sharp knife or shears to facilitate water uptake, then immediately plunge them into tepid water to condition them for arranging. Split woody stems; don't mash them. Mashing crushes the fibers so that the stems won't take up water.

❦ Strip off any foliage that falls below the water line; it will rot and sour the water.

❦ Using a florist's conditioning solution can lengthen the life of your bouquets. Or experiment with what's on hand; some gardeners suggest adding aspirin, pennies, or lemony soft drinks to the water. What's effective is the right balance of acid, sugar for nutrition, and bleach for controlling bacteria. If you use a floral conditioner, measure it carefully; don't use too much. Changing the water daily also can help refresh cut flowers.

❦ Some flowers drink more than others. Keep an eye on the water level and at the same time remove dead blossoms.

ARRANGING FLOWERS

❦ Pick plenty of flowers so that you have extras to play with. Your creativity will bloom as you get close to natural colors and forms. Be dramatic, classic, or whimsical. Try a single flower. Try contrasts such as small and large flowers, smooth and fuzzy textures, and complementary colors.

❦ Move beyond vases. Anything that holds water can hold flowers, and some of the most eye-catching arrangements are those in teapots, wineglasses, mugs, crocks, cans, and baskets (with inserts).

❦ Mix it up. Combine tall flowers with full ones, branches with smooth-stemmed blooms. Use plenty of white to add light to bouquets, and add foliage from flowers and other plants.

❦ Don't crowd the flowers into a bunch. Leave room so that they can show off.

❦ If your flowers need support, use a flower-arranging "frog" (easy to find at flea markets or garage sales), a layer of clean pebbles, or florist's foam.

> *Have you ever noticed that a bouquet of tulips closes at night and opens again in the morning? Cut tulips are far from static. They stretch toward light, stems elongating up to about three inches after they are cut, and their blossoms may double in size.*
>
> — *The Old Farmer's Almanac*
>   *Gardener's Companion, 1996*

Flowers for Dyeing

Before synthetic dye pigments were
produced in the mid-19th century,
dyes were often made from
plants and flowers. Growing
the flowers best suited for
dyeing is a wonderful way
to remember that ancient art
and try your hand at natural
dyeing. At the same time,
you'll have a beautiful garden
and armloads of flowers
for bouquets.

Lily of the valley
(*Convallaria* spp.)

FLOWER	COLOR OF DYE
Black-eyed Susan (*Rudbeckia fulgida*)	Green
Cosmos (*Cosmos sulphureus*)	Reddish orange
Golden Marguerite (*Anthemis tinctoria*)	Yellow, yellowish green
Goldenrod (*Solidago* spp.)	Yellow, yellowish green
Lily of the valley (*Convallaria* spp.)	Green
Marigold (*Calendula* spp.)	Yellow
Tansy (*Tanacetum* spp.)	Yellow, yellowish green
Tickseed (*Coreopsis tinctoria*)	Gold, reddish brown, mahogany

The Floral Calendar

To everything there is a season,
and a time to every purpose under the Heaven.

— Ecclesiastes, 3:1

The succession of the seasons in the garden has always suggested a calendar, and certain months have come to be associated with certain flowers and plants. In rural societies and folk cultures the world over, social traditions, farm chores, and garden events are linked to certain months, and this cycle of events has been the inspiration for many almanacs, indispensable to our forebears and useful guides for us today.

JANUARY
The Midwinter Month

CARNATION
"If in January, the sun much appear
March and April pay full dear."

❧

FEBRUARY
The Month of Purification

PRIMROSE
"A good farmer should have on
Candlemas Day
Half his turnips, and half his hay."

MARCH
The Month of New Life

VIOLET
"March damp and warm
Doth the farmer much harm
But a March without water
Dowers the farmer's daughter."

❧

APRIL
The Spring Cuckoo's Month

DAISY
"This April, with his stormy showers
Doth make the earth yield
pleasant flowers."

❧

MAY
The Month of Milk and May Games

LILY OF THE VALLEY
"A swarm in May
Is worth a load of hay."

❧

JUNE
The Midsummer Month

ROSE
"June damp and warm
Doth the farmer no harm."

JULY
The Month of Haymaking

WATER LILY
*"In this month of July, eschew all
wanton bed-sports,
and of all things forbear Lettuce."*

∽๐∾

AUGUST
The Month of Harvest and Weeds

GLADIOLUS
*"Make sure of your reapers,
get harvest in hand
The corn that is ripe, doth but
shed as it stand."*

∽๐∾

SEPTEMBER
The Month of Plenty

MORNING GLORY
*"September blow soft
Until the apples be in the loft."*

∽๐∾

OCTOBER
*The Month of Fruit and
Falling Leaves*

CALENDULA
*"In October, dung your field
And all your land its wealth
will yield."*

NOVEMBER
The Month of Blood and Bonfires

CHRYSANTHEMUM
*"If Martinmas ice will bear a duck
Then look for a winter of slush
and muck."*

∽๐∾

DECEMBER
The Month of Christmas

POINSETTIA
*"No season to hedge
Get beetle and wedge
Cleave logs now all
For kitchen and hall."*

Carnation
(Dianthus spp.*)*

A Taste for Edible Flowers

For some of us, flowers are too pretty *not* to eat, so we munch on marigolds, nibble nasturtiums, and decorate our wedding cakes with violets.

Why eat flowers? For sustenance, we choose shoots, roots, and leaves. Aside from a desire to be considered avant-garde, we value edible flowers for the color they add to salads and other dishes, the elegance they contribute to a dish's presentation, and their taste.

All the more reason to grow your own — and to be scrupulously careful in picking blossoms to pile on your plate. Not just any flower will do; you must choose those that are (first and foremost) grown without pesticides and botanically safe to eat. Potent natural chemicals abide in many innocent-looking plants. Petunias, for example, appear on many lists of edible flowers, despite records that Ecuadorian Indians used them in their religious ceremonies to induce a heady sensation of flight.

Poison hemlock *(Conium maculatum)*, the very plant that killed Socrates, resembles its close relative Queen Anne's lace, or wild carrot *(Daucus carota)*, and is naturalized in both North and South America. In at least one case, overzealous kitchen assistants have gathered it to add variety to salads.

Knowing the correct botanical names of plants recommended for eating and their chemical properties is essential for the gardener who wants to grow edible flowers. Make a positive identification of any unfamiliar plant you want to eat, then check it out in a reliable source book. Elderberries are traditionally used to make fritters and syllabubs, but some species are poisonous. Although recipes for rhododendrons exist, most of the 400 species are very poisonous — only a few can be eaten. Rose petals are edible, but which are tasty enough to warrant eating?

The flowers of all culinary herbs are edible and offer a variety of tastes. Thyme, sage, basil, rosemary, arugula, and fennel have distinct, interesting flavors. One gardener described the taste of anise hyssop *(Agastache foeniculum)* as "candy"; another reports that it tastes like licorice-laced root

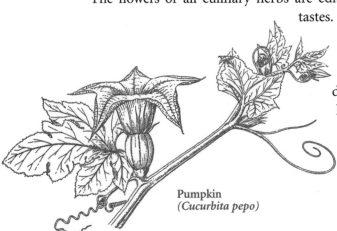

Pumpkin
(Cucurbita pepo)

beer. Pale lavender chive *(Allium schoenoprasum)* and white garlic chive *(A. tuberosum)* blossoms taste oniony; blue borage blossoms *(Borago officinalis)* are a bit fuzzy but taste pleasantly of cucumbers. Rosemary flowers *(Rosmarinus officinalis)* have a refreshing piny flavor much like their leaves, and English lavender *(Lavandula angustifolia)* has a sweet lemony floral taste, although other species taste medicinal.

Beautiful, bright-colored nasturtiums *(Tropaeolum majus)* are among the most versatile edible flowers, lending a peppery watercress-like flavor to salads, vegetable dishes, and herb butters. Some daylily blossoms *(Hemerocallis* spp.) are tasty in a pleasant floral way; others taste metallic. Squash blossoms *(Cucurbita* spp.) are sizable enough to stuff with cheese or sauté for a pasta sauce.

Not surprisingly, most flowers have a floral flavor. Apple blossoms *(Malus* spp.) have a delicate floral taste; sweet violets *(Viola odorata)* have a stronger floral taste. Tufted violets *(V. cornuta)*, pansies *(V. wittrockiana)*, and Johnny-jump-ups *(V. tricolor)* have a light flowery flavor. Roses have a variety of tastes, but *Rosa rugosa* 'Alba', *R. eglanteria*, and *R. damascena* are said to be the most flavorful, ranging from mild to lush, and can be used for flavoring sweets or sorbets. Lilac blossoms *(Syringa vulgaris)* are edible and have a sweet floral taste. So do pinks *(Dianthus* spp.), with a hint of clove. Chrysanthemums *(Chrysanthemum × morifolium)* have been used in Chinese cuisine for centuries but have a pungent, slightly bitter flavor; use them for garnish.

Perhaps your gardening plans include planting a bed of edible flowers near the kitchen door. Most of these are easily grown from seed (except rosemary, apple blossoms, and roses) and are suited to a variety of garden situations. Examine blossoms after you pick them, remove any insects or dirt, and then use them in moderation in salads or soups or lavishly to garnish a plate. When you do so, you will be both part of a long and honorable tradition of gardening for flavor and on the cutting edge.

The most important thing to remember about edible flowers is to be fully familiar with them. Don't go around the garden nibbling at everything — some flowers are poisonous — and make sure they're organically grown.

— David Hirsch, Ithaca, New York

Everlastings

Anyone who hates to see summer end should cut and dry an assortment of flowers and herbs for winter bouquets. A colorful wreath or arrangement of dried flowers can add beauty to a room, make an elegant gift, and help carry a gardener through until planting season.

Even if you haven't planted flowers specifically for drying, many popular garden stalwarts can be dried successfully. "If you can grow it, you can dry it," says one Zone 3 gardener. Take a look around your own garden for appealing shapes and colors you'd like to preserve. It's true that colors change when petals dry, but the softer, more muted colors are lovely, too, and the shapes of plants that produce seedpods or feathery fronds can be very dramatic in a dried bouquet.

Another intriguing possibility is drying wildflowers — if you are lucky enough to live near a field of goldenrod or along a road bordered with black-eyed Susans, wild white yarrow, rabbit-foot clover, or handsome grasses. All of these dry well, either in flower or seed.

HARVESTING: TIMING IS EVERYTHING

The key to success with dried flowers is simple and yet specific: harvest them at just the right time. It's important to harvest flowers before they're pollinated, when the plant is still sending sugars to the opening blossoms. These sugars will help hold the blossom together after the petals have dried. In most cases, this is just before the flower is fully open. (Flowers usually open a bit more as they dry.) You also might try harvesting flowers at different stages of maturity, for variety. Don't bother to dry flowers that are diseased, insect damaged, or past their prime.

Black-eyed Susan
(*Rudbeckia hirta*)

For best results, cut flowers with a sharp knife or shears on a dry, sunny day, in mid- to late morning. The perfect time is just after the dew has evaporated from petals and leaves but before the sun is hot enough to dilute the essential oils that give herbs and flowers their characteristic scents. The flowers must be completely dry when you pick them. Strip off lower leaves so that they won't interfere with air circulation, and keep the stems long — a foot or more if possible. (You can always cut them to size.) Carry a bucket with you, and plunge the stems into tepid water to keep them fresh until you're ready to dry them. Protect them from strong sun, too. Start the drying process as soon as you can, for flowers are less likely to rot if they're dried quickly.

DRYING: HEADS DOWN!
Air-drying flowers is as easy as it sounds. Gather flowers into small bunches, fasten them together, and hang them. Most flowers dry best hanging upside down. Papery, deep-orange Chinese lantern plant (winter cherry) is an exception; these flowers must be dried standing so that the pods will droop naturally. Grasses, too, look best when dried standing.

Ideally, flowers would be hung separately to dry, so that air can circulate around them, but this isn't really necessary, except for really big flowers such as peonies or hydrangeas. Group flowers in small bunches (five to ten flowers, no more than a dozen) secured by an elastic band. Elastic is better than string or wire because it tightens as the stems shrink.

PRESERVATION: UNDER THE EAVES
Hang bunches of flowers in a warm, dark, dry place, or at least out of strong light, which bleaches colored flowers. The attic, an upstairs room, a closet, or even a dry cellar is fine, but keep them away from windows and avoid outdoor sheds or garages, which get damp at night. Shelter them inside a paper bag if you have no dark place for them.

If you live in a cool, damp climate, be sure to find a drying place that's warmed by a stove or hot-water pipe and well ventilated. The flowers will absorb any moisture in the air, and they may mold. A low-powered fan to stir the air is a plus.

Keep in mind that flowers and herbs look and smell wonderful while they're drying. Consider them part of your interior décor as they hang in bunches along shelves in the dining room or kitchen (away from steam or spray), off the backs of chairs, or on an antique laundry or towel rack. The sight of drying flowers is one of life's simple pleasures.

OTHER DRYING METHODS

Less romantic but faster than air-drying is processing flowers in a microwave oven. Arrange thin blossoms loosely inside a paper towel; set thicker ones in a microwave-proof dish and cover with a towel. Dry for one to two minutes at high power, then let the flowers cool for at least ten minutes. Dry only a few flowers at a time and watch closely to make sure they don't overdry.

Silica gel, a common desiccant in dry, granular form, is another option. It is fairly expensive but can be reused for years. Most silica gel is colored with a moisture-indicating feature so that you can tell when it has extracted moisture from flowers. Most flowers will dry in five to ten days with silica, which works well with flowers such as daffodils and tulips that don't air-dry well. Soft-petaled flowers dried with silica retain a strong color and often look very dramatic.

Grandmother's Garden

I remember it with great affection as a sunny lovely place. There was a 30-foot terrace garden halfway down the hill full of bright flowers for cutting. I remember roses and gladioli in profusion, and I grow them today because they remind me of my grandmother. She loved to be out there handling the earth and the flowers. And I remember a rose arbor, painted white. That's the thing about gardening — it has so many emotional associations.

— Susan Gordon, Tenafly, New Jersey

Appendix

A Garden Journal

I have often thought that if Heaven had given me choice of my position
and calling, it should have been on a rich spot of earth, well watered,
and near a good market for the productions of the garden. No occupation
is so delightful to me as the culture of the earth, and no culture
comparable to that of the garden . . . I am still devoted to the garden.
But though an old man, I am but a young gardener.

— Thomas Jefferson (1743–1826)

It is true; we are all young gardeners. There is always something new to learn: ideas and recommendations from other gardeners, new plants to try or new techniques for growing old favorites, an infinite number of aesthetic combinations, ingenious methods for pest control, and, of course, the perennial challenge of variable weather from year to year. Each plant in your garden has its own particular needs, and keeping track of those needs is very often the key to success.

Thomas Jefferson saw great benefit in keeping a garden journal. His "Garden Book" contains entries from 1766 to 1824 — some 58 years! In it, he made observations about his plants, recorded new additions and sources, and jotted down informal reminders to himself regarding maintenance of the gardens and grounds of his home, Monticello.

Since most gardeners would rather spend their time gardening than writing about gardening, a garden journal should afford a quick and simple method of recording useful information for future reference. In the pages that follow, we offer a form that allows you to keep a record of your garden plants. In addition, we provide a month-by-month calendar for plotting out your gardening tasks (when to order seeds, start seedlings, and so on) and making seasonal observations (e.g., frost dates, what blooms when, and the like). Enjoy!

Plant Name	Type*	Date Planted	Notes

*Type: A = Annual, P= Perennial, B= Bulb

Plant Name	Type*	Date Planted	Notes

*Type: A = Annual, P= Perennial, B= Bulb

Garden Calendar

January	February
March	April
May	June

July	October
August	November
September	December

Seed & Plant Sources

NAME _____   PHONE _____

ADDRESS _____   FAX _____

NOTES _____

_____

_____

NAME _____   PHONE _____

ADDRESS _____   FAX _____

NOTES _____

_____

_____

NAME _____   PHONE _____

ADDRESS _____   FAX _____

NOTES _____

_____

_____

NAME _____   PHONE _____

ADDRESS _____   FAX _____

NOTES _____

_____

_____

Index